HOW TO BE A 3% MAN

Winning the Heart of the Woman of Your Dreams

By Corey Wayne

HONOR

This book is dedicated to the American soldier. No matter whether the cause is popular or not, I am in awe of the fact that when their country calls them, they go, and they go willingly. They take our place on the battlefield, risking everything they have, because it is part of who they are. They all are my heroes and I owe all of my success, happiness, and opportunities to past, present, and future generations of their kind. May God keep them safe and speed the day to us when their sacrifice is no longer required because humanity has learned that the real enemy is hatred itself and the way to real happiness is unconditional love. Until that day comes I take great pride and comfort in knowing they will continue to stand up and show us what real honor and integrity is. I dedicate my life to helping bring humanity closer together, and always giving my gifts to the world in hopes that I may honor all of their collective sacrifices so they are not in vain.

ACKNOWLEDGEMENTS

I would like to thank my mother who taught me to be so determined and never give up no matter what. I would also like to thank Tony Robbins for being such a great leader and mentor in my life. I would also like to thank my dad for teaching me the difference between right and wrong. I am grateful for the close relationship we have today – I love you very much. I also would like my brother Chris to know how proud I am to have you as my brother. All you have gone through to achieve your dreams is inspiring to me. I love you very much.

For all the women in my life who have helped me become the man I am today: *I am grateful*. You know who you are.

I would also like to express my gratitude to you, the reader. You are embarking on a journey that will change the world. By becoming the loving person you are inside and being comfortable with that person, you unconsciously give permission to all others to do the same. Your children will grow up in a household where they get to see first hand what a truly unconditional, loving relationship is like. Therefore they will go out into the world and model your success. This will continue to impact society for generations to come and start reducing the amount of dysfunctional relationships that exist today.

The benefits will be too far reaching to imagine. The surface benefits will be happier kids, aunts, uncles, grandparents, parents, teachers, workers, etc., which will translate into less crime, less hate, more understanding, and a world that continues to come closer and closer together in love until one day hatred becomes a thing of the past. The light always scatters the darkness. The higher energy of love always replaces the lower energies of hate and resentment.

Table of Contents

Part I: In the Beginning

Introduction

The beginning. That is the place where men need to get back to in order to make the changes needed to win the heart of the woman of their dreams. It is time to go back and decide what you really want, who you really are, and what you plan to do with the wealth of information that I will be teaching you throughout this book.

As the story goes, in the beginning there was only one man, Adam, and there was one special lady, Eve, created just for him. Life would be so much simpler if that were the case for us today. No muss and fuss of dating, no worry that our lady is going to walk out the door and into the arms of another man – there was no other man.

Here is the greatest thing about this book. While you may not be able to "create" that one special lady just for you, I am going to teach you what to look for in a woman and how to find and attract the woman that you ideally want. When you finally do meet her, I am going to teach you how to approach her. You will learn what to say and especially what *not* to say to turn her off. Basically, what I will be teaching you is the art of being a 3% man.

The next obvious question is: *Okay, what is a 3% man?* This is a very important concept in that you will be learning over the course of this book. I am not trying to tell you to be only 3% man and open the rest of your masculinity to explore your feminine side. The 3% man is one of the 3 men out of 100 that a woman meets and is drawn to because he understands who she is and better yet, understands who *he* is. In life, usually the top 3% in any field or area make most of the money, enjoy most of the success, have the best toys, date the most beautiful people and generally live the kind of lives most people only dream of.

Why does being in this 3% matter? Simply stated, it matters because these are the men that women are drawn to. One of the most important things to understand when you meet a woman is that women love mystery. They love a guy that is his own man despite what others think about him or who he should be. They love a guy that is confident and goes for what he wants in life without fear. They want a man that is centered, one that is in control of himself, has purpose, and knows where he is going. A woman wants a man she can't have her way with, and no matter what she says or does, she is not going to be able to sway him from his path or from his purpose in life.

A true Alpha Male, a man who goes for what he wants and has positive expectations that he will achieve his goals, will choose his purpose and his passion over a woman if faced with the choice. Masculine energy, after all, is about purpose, drive, mission, succeeding, accomplishing, breaking thru barriers, achieving goals, etc.

Be honest, gentlemen, if you did not care at all, you would not have picked up this book. Obviously, something is not working with what you are already doing. Women love men that understand them and how attraction works. If you ask most guys if they understand women, they look at you like you are speaking a foreign language. Most guys are clueless in that department. The sad reality is, most men are talking women right out of dating them, sleeping with them, having a relationship with them, etc. because they simply have no idea what creates attraction and what turns a woman off.

What this book will do for you is to give you more than just a clue. It will give you a whole new insight into understanding women. The subtle differences that make the difference in attracting women. I will take you through the process of understanding, step-by-simple-step. This book was designed to give you the answers to the questions you have about women regarding pickup techniques, dating skills, relationship skills, communication, attraction, sex, etc.

Think of this book as a coaching manual that gives you the baseline knowledge of how to interact with women successfully. Throughout the book I will give you search terms you can Google that will bring up specific articles and YouTube videos on my website that go into more detail of the essential skills, techniques and knowledge related to specific parts of this book. Many of the articles on my website have the actual emails included from other readers/viewers. I have analyzed and diagnosed their emails and inserted my comments in them so you can learn from where they went wrong. Since most people find out about my book from my website and the fact that I have created thousands of articles and videos since publishing the first edition of this book, it's easier to reference them throughout this book instead of trying to incorporate them all here.

I will take you from your initial meeting to making love for the first time. This book will help to lift the cloudy haze that surrounds the mysteries of the pickup, dating and relationship world, understanding women, and will give you clear insight into achieving your goals.

I will explain why women fall for the jerks and blow off the nice guys. You will learn to understand the meaning of everything she says to you. You will learn that women tend to be driven by emotion and connection instead of logic and reason like men are. Feminine energy is about opening up to receive love, bonding, connection, etc. Women are physically, emotionally, mentally and spiritually designed to receive a man. I will take you from the initial moment of meeting your dream lady to the day you walk down the aisle to get married and live happily ever after, if that's your goal. You can also use what I teach to meet and date lots of different women until you figure out what you really want. The best is yet to come. I will also teach you, once you land Mrs. Right, how to keep her madly in love with you so that you *do* live happily ever after.

In this book you will learn things that many women do not even understand about themselves. Why do women say they want one thing and then respond to another? Most important of all, I will teach you how to win the heart of the beautiful woman of your dreams. That is not a misprint. If you allow yourself to take my guidance and are willing to learn, I will give you the skills and tools to help you finally understand women and have the relationship of your dreams.

The wonderful truth is that if you treat a woman properly and allow her to come to you at her own pace with minimal and simple actions on your part, she will do most of the chasing, calling, texting & pursuing! That allows you to focus on what's most important in any man's life, your mission and purpose! Ironically, the more you focus on and passionately pursue your purpose in life, the more attractive women will find you in general. A man pursuing a purpose he has a burning desire to accomplish gives off a much happier, peaceful, relaxed, successful, inviting, confident and positive vibe than a guy who hates his job, his life and his circumstances.

What you will learn from me is what only about 3 out of every 100 men know, and that is how to understand women. Once you understand and apply the principles in this book to your dating and relationships, you will be in the top 3% of men out there. You can be confident that you will have little or no competition when you finally target the woman of your desires. Especially when you can notice and see first hand with your own eyes and ears how badly the average guy is blowing it with women. Google "Corey Wayne Why You Have No Competition."

You do not have to look like Brad Pitt to own the heart of a beautiful woman. If you are single, there is an amazingly beautiful woman out there, desperate to meet the man you really are on the inside. I will teach you how to become balanced, centered, and confident with women, and to no longer be intimidated by them, even the beautiful ones. You will learn that you MUST treat all women the same. As a matter of fact, a big reason why guys fail with women they have a perfectly good chance of seducing is because they treat women they like and want differently than women they don't. They put women on a pedestal and treat them like a celebrity instead of a real human being. They act like they are unworthy of her and don't even realize that they're doing it! Women have no choice but to agree with their bad behavior and reject them.

Some of the things I will teach you in order to become successful with women may seem the opposite of what you think you should do. If you want to meet and own the heart of the woman of your dreams, or get your wife to fall back in love with you, then this book is the key to that kingdom. These principles apply to women everywhere in the world, regardless of their location or culture. I coach men from all over the world and from some of the most conservative societies. Guess what? Women and men respond emotionally to what they respond to, no matter where they live or what their cultural background is.

Becoming successful with women starts before you ever even meet a woman that you want to date. You first need to learn how to attract the right woman into your life. Once you meet her, you have to know what to say, what not to say, and how to get her contact information so you can later call and take her out on a date, or... if you're really confident you can make a date the moment you meet her. You want to take measured, consistent steps with women, practice what I teach and take risks based upon your own comfort level. "Progress always involves risk. You can't steal second base & keep your foot on first." ~ Frederick Wilcox.

Then comes the next step – how long after you get her information should you wait to call? Do you call her the next day? Do you wait a week? Do you call her in two days? Make a date on the spot? What do you do? My goal with the techniques and strategies I teach is to give you plenty of tools for your pickup, dating and relationship toolbox. Once you understand the mindset and actions a man should take, the words really don't matter. It is HOW you say things rather than what you say that matters.

From the time you meet your lady to the point where you've been together for ten years or more, you are always going to be gauging what her level of attraction to you is, and what her emotional attraction to you is. The simple principle that all this is based upon is that when women have a high level of attraction, they help you. In other words, if you just met a woman and you want to ask her out on a date, she is going to help you get to her front door or meet up for a date. She will make it easy for you.

Adam Carolla, the comedian, says that when a woman likes you, she starts opening her doors and all you have to do is walk through them, but if they start closing in your face you simply walk away. The key is to know when to walk away and when to take action. Guys who fail with women tend to chase and pursue too much to the point of appearing like a stalker when they sense a woman pulling away. Google "Corey Wayne Act Like A Stalker… Get Rejected." I like to call this "the illusion of action." They falsely believe that by taking action they will make something happen. Unfortunately, all that happens is that they make the girl go away and start ignoring them.

The lower her level of attraction is, the harder it is going to be to get to her front door or meet up for a date, if at all. So throughout this process of going back to the beginning and re-learning how to approach women, you will be learning what to say, how to say it, and you will know how to respond to her questions and her tests. Make no mistake – all women test. They test because they want to know what it is that you are made of. They want to know that if they push you or lean on you, that you are not going to fall over and cave in to what they want. Google "Corey Wayne Women Bluff To Test Your Strength."

They want you to act like more of a man than they do. A man is supposed to be the leader and gently lead the interaction to where he wants it to go. Ultimately, a man and a woman who like each other eventually end up having sex. That is after all, the object of seduction. The purpose of a date is to create a fun filled romantic opportunity for sex to happen. Biologically, men and women are driven to mate with the most dominant member of the opposite sex. Attractive and healthy bodies are indicative of people with strong genes who will produce strong offspring that can survive to adulthood and reproduce. This perpetuates another successful generation with the family genes being passed on. I will teach you the behaviors, body language, physiology and words of a dominant male so you can start succeeding with women like never before.

On my website (UnderstandingRelationships.com) and YouTube Channel (CoachCoreyWayne) I discuss questions from people just like you who are implementing what I teach. I critique their game by commenting on what they are doing right, what they are doing wrong and what they need to do in the future to improve. I encourage you to sign up for my FREE eNewsletter on my website or subscribe to my YouTube Channel to fine tune your approach.

Why This Book Was Written

Let me ask you a few questions and see whether or not they hit close to home for you:

- Are you one of those guys that has said more than once: *Why is it that the women I want never want me, and the ones I don't want are crazy about me?*

- Have you met a beautiful woman that you just *knew* was your soulmate, but she would never give you your first date or go out with you on a second date?

- Have you ever asked a woman why she would not go out with you and she never gives you what seems to be a straight answer?

- Have you ever felt that a woman really liked you and she even gave you her phone number, but then would never go out with you?

- Have you ever had women flake on you and cancel dates at the last minute for BS reasons?

- Do you feel like women have been giving you the run around?

- Have you ever had a girlfriend say to you: *"Can we just be friends? We need to take a break. I'm confused, etc."* when you thought everything was going great?

- Has she ever said she just wanted to be friends after telling you a few weeks before that she loved you?

- Do you have a hot girl "friend" that you would like to turn into a girlfriend? Google "Corey Wayne How To Turn A Friend Into A Girlfriend" and "Corey Wayne Stuck In The Friendship Zone? How To Turn A Girl

Friend Into A Girlfriend" and "Corey Wayne Asking Friends To Become Girlfriends."

- Are you in a relationship that is not going well and you have no clue how to turn it around?

- Has your wife or girlfriend of how ever many years stopped being the feminine woman you fell in love with?

- Has your wife or girlfriend ever uttered those fateful words: *You **never** listen to me?*

- Has your wife left you and you are still trying to figure out what the hell happened?

- Has a woman ever said things to you that just do not make sense?

- Has your girlfriend or wife ever said it was okay for you to do something and then you did it and she was pissed off?

- Are you totally confused about women and feel as though you do not have a clue how to understand them?

- Have you ever had a woman break a date and tell you she really wanted to see you, but you could never seem to coordinate that date to go out with her?

- Have you ever made a date with a lady and she told you to call before you came to pick her up, and then could never get her to pick up her phone again?

- Do you feel like women in general do not make any sense, that they say one thing and do another, or make you feel as though they like you and then never will go out with you?

- Do you feel like nothing you do seems to make your lady happy even when you do what she says she wants?

- After all your years of dating do you feel like you still have never been able to get the type of lady you know in your heart you really want and deserve?

- Are you a really nice guy that always gets dumped for the bad boy by your ladies? Google "Corey Wayne Why Nice Guys Finish Last" and "Nice Guy Finishes Last… Again" and "You're Too Much Of A Nice Guy."

- Have you ever seen a drop dead gorgeous woman with a man that is… well let's say *challenged* in the looks department and wondered to yourself: *How did he do that?*

This book is for those guys that have met a woman and could not ever seem to get to her front porch or meet her for a first date. It is for those guys that have maybe met a woman, went out on a first date and thought everything was great, but then cannot seem to ever get her on the phone again. It is for those guys who have met a woman they *thought* seemed really interested and she gave them a phone number, but then they cannot seem to get her on the phone, she has lame excuses as to why she can't see him this week, or she is always busy. It is for those guys that may have been dating a woman for a while and were spending a lot of time together, but then all of the sudden she started cutting the dates short, she starts calling/texting/messaging less and less, she has other things going on, or she is just not as available as she used to be.

This book is also for guys that are married. The first thing a 3% man learns is that the courtship never stops. Google "Corey Wayne The Courtship Never Ends." This book is for those guys that may have been married for some time and now your wife does not ever want to touch you. It is for those guys that maybe want to take their wives out to dinner and find that their women never want to spend any time with them. It's for those guys who want to get the sexual attraction spark back in their relationship so their wives look at them with the same desire and interest that they used to.

I used to be one of those guys. Let me share *My Story*:

Growing up I remember having a lot of crushes on girls, but never getting the ones I wanted. When I tried to get the ones I wanted, my heart was usually stomped on. In high school, I would write letters to girls I liked or get my friends to ask them out for me. I was so scared of rejection I could barely talk to the ones I was really interested in. I felt completely inadequate around women in general. Google "Corey Wayne 3 Ways To Seduce Women."

Ever so slowly I overcame my fear of just talking to them and took the safe approach by repressing my feelings. I did not know it at the time, but when a guy holds back because he does not know what to say, is fearful or simply intimidated by women, flirting and talking with women becomes awkward and the women can feel it; this leads to rejection. My favorite approach back then? I decided to take the friendship route to their heart. I invested months in this process and when I could no longer take it, I would tell them how I really felt. For some strange reason they still wanted to just be friends.

At the time I did not get it. Let me rephrase that: *I did not have a clue!* My senior high school prom was interesting. I had a crush on a girl in my class who had a boyfriend. While at a party I asked another girl I liked to go to prom and her response was: *I don't know you very well.*

In my infinite wisdom, I tried to reason with her and convince her to say yes. I had yet to learn that women are emotional beings and like to connect and create rapport via conversation, similar experiences and emotions. Guys tend to be logic and reason driven. If a woman's emotions are not engaged, it will always be fruitless. My assurances that we would get to know each other at prom and that I had a lot of popular friends did not seem sway her. I could not understand her logic. My thought was: *Hey, I'm a Senior and she's only a Junior (my fallacy of using male logic and reason to get women to do what you want).*

It didn't make sense to me. Here's a clue, guys, her response actually meant: *No thank you, I am not interested in going out with you or getting to know you at all.* So why did she not just come right out and say that?

We'll get to that a little later. Back to prom: A friend of a friend set me up with yet another friend as a blind prom date. Well, once we pulled up in the limo to pick her up I realized she was much taller than I was. She was a volley ball player and a very nice girl, just like her friend said she was. We had fun together.

The next morning I realized why she set me up with her very tall friend. She had ulterior motives. My friend Carl's date had asked him to the prom. Carl had asked me to ask one of the cheerleaders that was a friend of mine to prom for him. She said: *No thanks.*

He was the type of friend that would do anything for anyone. He was a great guy, but unfortunately he knew as much about women as I did, which was nothing. The girl that went with Carl only wanted someone to go with; she had no real interest in him. Carl promptly decided to fall in love with her. Once we were all back at the hotel Carl got pretty upset when he tried to make his move and got rejected.

He had a lot to drink and kept going on and on about how he had been rejected by his date to everyone he saw.

Our senior class had the whole floor of the hotel. You can imagine what was going on with all those unsupervised drunk teenagers. Party like a rockstar! The next morning, I woke up to my feet being rubbed by the friend that had set me up with my prom date. She was dating another friend of mine and apparently had a crush on me.

At the time I thought: *Great, another one who wants me that I don't want, and the one I **do** want is with someone else.* I had a crush on someone else who had a boyfriend. That's pretty much how my life went on for a few years after that. I seemed to always want a girl that was unavailable or had no interest in me. I figured over time she would fall for me. If I could just be a nice enough guy, then she would like me. It never worked. Nice guys always seem to finish last. Why is that?

I kept trying to figure women out. I became better at approaching them with time, but back then I used alcohol to overcome my insecurities. In the next few paragraphs I have included brief stories of the ones I felt were turning points in my life or when I learned a great deal more that helped to lift the cloudy veil from my understanding of women.

When I was 24, I met a girl that was a friend of one of my best buddies. I was instantly enamored with her and better yet, she really seemed to like me. I got her number and called her at work and she said she would call me back later. The next day she actually *did* call me back. I was stunned. I had a live one!

She did a lot of the talking. I didn't say much at the time because I was in shock. I just kept asking questions because I wanted to know everything about her. She was fascinating to me! To me she was a perfect 10: Long, dark, straight hair, beautiful hazel eyes, very tan skin, 105 pounds and 5' 2". She was really sweet and friendly and very forward. She asked me if I wanted to go to lunch, and I told her I would have to check my schedule and get back to her.

I am kidding. I made plans right there on the spot. Tip: when a woman asks you out or suggests that you go on a date it means she has a high level of attraction for you.

I was a project engineer at the time for a construction company in Ft. Lauderdale, Florida, working on a project right on the ocean. She showed up for our date, on time, and in this unbelievably tight outfit with very short shorts that showed her amazingly heavenly figure off. She took my breath away, as well as that of everyone else sitting at the conference table in the onsite construction office.

I felt like I was walking on air as I casually strolled over to give her a hug. She smelled like candy. When we walked outside, she was chatting away and touching my arm (physical contact is another indicator of attraction a woman as for you. The higher her attraction the more she will want to have her hands on you). She just seemed so happy to be there with me. I was in shock and my stomach was in knots. We sat there and had lunch I was in awe. God had finally blessed me with the woman of my dreams, and one who amazingly enough seemed so interested in me.

After the date, I did nothing all afternoon except fantasize about how the rest of my life was going to be: Where we were going to live, how beautiful our kids were going to be, what it would be like making love to her, and on and on. How many times have you thought that way when meeting a woman who knocked your socks off? She called me later on that night and we talked for hours (what I should have done was get off the phone and set the next definite date. I would have built more sexual anticipation that way). As the days went by she just kept calling me and was really aggressive. We went out for lunch the next week and met out for drinks a few times. An important tip is to treat a woman like a lover always, never a friend or she will assume you are gay, weak, lack confidence, etc. and generally not a catch. If you act like a nice guy and do lunches and movies, but never make a physical move to kiss her, etc., usually by the second or third date you'll get the lets just be friends speech. Men who are successful and have choice with women, plan evening dates that can lead to sex at your place or hers. I like to call it a fun-filled romantic opportunity for sex to happen. That is, after all, the whole point of seduction. To get closer and closer to her until you end up inside of her.

I remember one night when I took another guy friend and met her out at a night club her father owned. She seemed to know everyone there. Every time we got to talking, someone else would take her away from our conversation. After a while my friend wanted to go somewhere else. He said she was jerking me around and that we should go. I hadn't seen her for a while, so we left. Early the next morning she called and asked: *Where did you go last night? I was looking everywhere for you.* My only thought was: *What?*

Agreeing to or making group dates with her or your friends almost always leads to you getting cock-blocked and rejected. I learned that lesson the hard way too many times. No group dates until she's officially your girlfriend and in love with you. It interferes with a woman's ability to bond with you emotionally. Women also are afraid of being labeled a slut by their friends. Therefore, if you plan group dates, her fear of being labeled a slut if she sleeps with you right away will get in the way of seducing her successfully.

The night before I had felt as though I was just another guy and she had lost interest in me. I put it off as a figment of my imagination and I was back in the game. Walking away had a positive effect on her attraction for me, but I did not understand this at the time. I later learned that it is a scientific fact that women are more attracted to men whose feelings are unclear. Google "Corey Wayne Science Proves Women Are More Attracted To Men Whose Feelings Are Unclear." This went on for a few more weeks until she stopped calling me. I called her and received no answer. The next day she called me at home and left a message to say she was calling me back. She knew I wasn't home and would be at work. She usually called my pager when she wanted to get hold of me.

Finally, she no longer returned my calls. I was devastated. My dream girl did not want me. I was stunned. I sent her flowers. She called to say thanks but then gave me an answer I didn't understand when I asked her to go out with me again. Needless to say, she no longer wanted anything to do with me. It hurt even more when I heard she was dating another guy. I thought: *How could she just toss me aside like that?* My nice guy approach and not making a move got me nowhere.

About six months later I met the girl who would become my first wife. We met on a Friday night. I was leaving our favorite hangout with my friend Sean, and a mutual friend of ours, P.K., ran after me to tell me that her friend Shane really had the **hots** for me and wanted to meet me. Sean and I walked back in and I confidently strode up to her.

I really wanted to leave, but I thought: *Hey, this cute girl really likes me.* So I gave her my business card and told her to call me. She replied: *I don't call guys, so here is your card back and I'll give you my phone number if you like.* I was a little surprised, but I took her number. I called her early the next week to ask her out and talked to her mother. I never heard back from her.

The following Friday I ran into P.K. again and she asked: *What ever happened with Shane?* I told her I had left a message with Shane's mother and never heard back from her. P.K. said: *I guarantee she did not get the message because her parents never tell her when someone calls for her.* She told me I needed to call her again.

Early the next week I called and actually got her on the phone. We made a date for that Thursday. We went out and had a really good time.

We dated for about a year and a half, and then I decided I wanted to move to Orlando because I just loved everything about the city. Everything was new and growing and I just felt like it was the place for me. Shane told me the only way she would move to Orlando is if we were engaged to get married. So I went ahead and bought an engagement ring.

After getting the ring, I remember feeling as though it was not the right thing to do, and that I was not ready to get married. I didn't want to lose my relationship with Shane and proposed anyway. Even afterwards I had doubts. After talking to my friends, I came to the conclusion that I just had cold feet. I was simply too weak to stand up for myself and be a man at that time.

We did get married, but it was a difficult marriage. I wasn't happy in my career and wanted to start my own business. Neither one of us was fulfilled in our relationship with each other. A little over a year after getting married we were down in Ft. Lauderdale at my friend Sean's wedding. I went out for a night on the town with P.K.'s husband and a friend of mine, Alan, while our wives stayed home.

We ran into two sisters we had gone to high school with. One of them I had had a huge crush on. We were both exploring spirituality and had an amazing conversation. She had been a cheerleader and I remember sitting there thinking about how I didn't feel this way about my wife. A few weeks later I decided it wasn't fair to either one of us to stay together. I was not giving her the love she deserved. It was the hardest thing I ever had to do, but I told her I did not want to stay together. We remained friends until she moved back home a few years later and we lost touch.

I was free, or so I thought. Free to find the type of woman I knew I really deserved and desperately wanted to be with. I did not date, or even want to date, for about six months. I just wanted to heal and get clear. I focused on my new business and personal growth.

When I felt ready, I started working on trying to find the type of woman I really wanted to be with. It was not long before I met one. From the moment I laid eyes on her she took my breath away. There was only one small problem. She had a boyfriend. I thought: *Just my luck. Yet another woman I want that is unavailable.*

Do you see a pattern here? I continued to date other women and about two years after meeting her, she became single again. I was at the bar where she worked and she was telling me that she had recently broken up with her boyfriend. I asked her for her number as usual and almost fell over when she gave it to me. I couldn't believe it. So I called her the next day and we set a date for a Saturday.

Years later I realized that I tended to fall for unavailable women because emotionally it felt exactly the same as my relationship with my mother. Both of my parents were emotionless zombies. No kissing, hugging, hand holding, I love yous, etc. between each other. They were the same way toward my brother and me. We got yelled at and smacked around when we upset them, but never heard, "I'm proud of you! Great job! I love you! Etc." We just got verbal and physical abuse when we were wrong, and mostly ignored the rest of the time. I love my parents, but as I got older I realized that they were pretty fucked up emotionally. They came from fucked up families also. However, I have forgiven them and I would not be who I am without their parenting, good and bad. It made me really tough and able to endure insults from anyone and overcome tremendous odds. That's helped me tremendously to persevere when things look hopeless. To find a way, not a way out when faced with challenges.

I took her out on my jet skis, which were at a friend's lakefront house. We rode around on the water all day, stopping at a lakeside restaurant for lunch. For only the second time in my life I was on a date with the type of woman I really wanted to be with. The day was perfect and I was on cloud nine. I started fantasizing again about the future, what our kids would be like, where we would live, and what a fabulous life I would have with her.

Well, she was leaving on vacation and would be gone for a week. So when I thought she would be back, I sent her an email. I didn't hear from her for a couple days. I thought she had blown me off. I was hurt, so I wrote a long nasty email accusing her of mistreating me and made an ass of myself. When she did finally get back in town, she sent a nasty email in return and told me to get lost. I tried apologizing for months afterwards but it did not do any good. She would not take my calls or return my emails. So there I was: Strike Two. I resolved not to get married again unless I found the type of woman I really wanted and knew I deserved.

When I was 30, I started picking through all the information I could get my hands on about how to understand women. Some of it went against everything I had believed to be right. My success with the ones I really wanted never got past the first few weeks, so I felt I had nothing to lose and everything to gain by trying some of the information out.

I read some of the books and website articles out there and thought: *Now I have it!* A guy whose work really helped open my eyes was Doc Love. His website is Doclove.com. I encourage you to buy his dating dictionary. You can download his kindle version or order a paperback one with CDs. I think its $100 bucks on his website with the CDs, and $29 bucks for just the kindle version on Amazon.com. I don't agree with everything he believes/teaches, and some things he teaches I've found to not be accurate, but he is mostly spot on and funny as hell. Doc helped me realize I could apply my sales skills to pre-qualifying a woman's interest before taking her out on a date to make sure she was really interested in me romantically. I went out and started applying the principles I learned in self-help, Doc's stuff and dozens of others, and was amazed at how my being a challenge, indifferent, making definite dates, using body language attraction skills, simple pickup approaches, seduction techniques, only using a phone to set dates and not to talk, asking questions, only calling a girl once per week for a date, etc. had a positive effect on the ladies' attraction level. I dated one woman who claimed to have posed for Playboy. On our first date, she showed me the pictures to get my opinion, expecting me to drool. I thought to myself: *Oh, my – those can't be real!* I maintained my composure and said they were nicely done.

After a few weeks, I realized that although she was physically a 10, everything else in her life was not exactly what I was looking for. I never called her again. She was a mess. She lived with her ex husband and their kids. The house was always a mess. She was never ready when I went to pick her up, etc. For the first time, *I* blew off a beautiful woman. Now I started thinking that I really understood women and was a little full of myself. A few weeks later, I met a girl who just blew me away. I was intoxicated with her beauty and sex appeal. I looked her right in the eyes the night we met and said with 100% certainty, "you're intoxicating to look at." She was and still is to this day one of the most beautiful, sexy, charming and fun women on the planet.

We dated for a few weeks, and then things started getting a little squirrelly. She started out calling me everyday, and I acted as though I knew what was really going on, even though I still had a lot to learn. Then she became less available and started telling me things that didn't make any sense when I asked her out. One example I remember is: *I'm not sure where I am able to be at this time in my life.* I thought to myself: *What the hell does that mean?* She told me about an operation she might have to have and other things going on that were supposedly hindering her spending time with me. She never did have the operation and I heard from mutual friends that she had been out on the town with an ex-boyfriend. What was really going on was I was starting to over-pursue, be too available, talk on the phone too much instead of in person, letting her walk all over me, etc.

Why You Need To Read This Book More Than Once

So I picked up my stack of books again, and must have read through them 15 times. I found that I had missed a lot of information. Studies show that people retain only 7-10% of what they read after reading it. That is why I am going to recommend you read this book 10-15 times if you really want to understand this material and have the relationship of your dreams. Repetition is the mother of skill and you must understand all aspects of pickup, dating and relationships to be successful long term. Guys who read my book, website articles, newsletters and videos, but who are still are having problems; usually don't know the material in this book well enough.

I started applying the material I learned in earnest. It took about a month and a half of playing it cool until she went out with me again. It took me a year and a half to master the tools and techniques and get her to fall in love with me. I had finally done it. I got the lady of my dreams. We dated for about two years, and I was a part of her daughter's life for many years after we broke up. Her daughter is all grown up now, and I can't believe how this tiny little 5 year old I carried in my arms is now an adult! Kids change your life and she changed mine.

After going through this whole process, I learned some valuable lessons about myself. My own insecurities and doubts about being enough of a man to attract the lady of my dreams had all been an illusion. What you fear you attract, but what you look at disappears. I no longer feared beautiful women and was a completely centered and confident man. I notice as I walk around, whether in the mall, or grocery store, or wherever, I now get a lot of looks from women, whereas before they never seemed to notice. It's all about carrying yourself with your chest out, your head back and a feeling of being proud of yourself. Later in this book I will go into extensive detail about body language that attracts women and how to emulate it, but using proper body language, facial expressions and voice tone will make you appear to give off the same vibe and energy as the captain of the football team does. Google "Corey Wayne Body Language That Attracts Women." It's walking and acting exactly like a dominant alpha male walks. Everyone can feel when a dominant male or female walks into a room. It's like moths to a light bulb!

Women have invisible radar that can feel a confident, centered man approaching. It's an amazing feeling to be able to walk up to any woman I want and strike up a conversation. It has been a long journey to get to this place. The next lady I met became my girlfriend for a year. With her I had an amazing relationship from the start.

Back in October 2004, I sat down and made my list of the ideal woman that I wanted to bring into my life. In December 2004, about six weeks later, I went to a week-long Tony Robbins event in Palm Springs, California called: *Date with Destiny.*

I remember walking in and they had these little ping pong balls. You would write your name on it and they assigned you a number. This was for various drawings that they would be holding during the duration of the event. When you went to put it into the tumbler, they told you: *Put a good intention behind it!* The only prize I really wanted was to bring a new woman into my life – a soulmate. That was the intention that I put into my ball as I threw it into the tumbler.

The next day, which was actually the first day of the event, I saw this girl walk in. She was stunning and tiny, about 5'2. She just sort of strode into the room and sat down in the front row. I was sitting directly behind her. At that point, I didn't get much of a glimpse of her face, but her body was perfect. Her pants were so tight that they looked to be painted on her, and she had the most perfect figure I had ever seen in my entire life. I later learned she was a former Miss Figure winner.

At a Tony Robbins event, every 20-30 minutes or so, he has the participants stand up, stretch out, and get the blood flowing to keep the participants alert and awake to the information they are receiving. It was during a stretch break that she stood up and turned around, making eye contact with me. She had these big, beautiful brown eyes and long, straight blond hair. To me, she was physically perfect – everything that I had put on my list just six weeks before. I knew instantly that she was interested and that I was going to get to know her. Unfortunately, she left before the event was over the first night, so we didn't get a chance to meet. The event lasted five days and there were only 1500 people attending, so I knew we would meet again before the event was over.

The next night I was coming out of the dining room of a restaurant at the hotel and there she was talking to her uncle, who was a friend of mine. At the time, I had no idea they were related. I went over and started talking to my friend, and noticed her looking at me the whole time. She was eagerly hoping we would talk. She wanted me and it was written all over her face. I finally turned and asked her name, and then she asked mine. She also told me that she had noticed me sitting behind her the day before, and described what I had been wearing. That, in and of itself told me that she was very attracted to me.

With her eye contact, her body language, her attention to me, and many other little signs, I knew without a doubt that she had that high level of attraction. I had come to a place in my life where I had been living these things for so long that my own personal radar was sharp. I also somehow knew she was single. This is the place you can get to, if you follow this material. It's a place where you don't have to think about it any more, it just becomes a part of who and what you are. You walk around with this total air of confidence, and women will notice.

As David DeAngelo says, "Attraction is not a choice." He offers some good dating products I found out about after I had written the first edition of this book. His website is DoubleYourDating.com.

A woman knows in about 3 seconds if you make the cut or not. You must be a 5 or better on a scale of 1 to 10 in order to have a chance to date her. If you are a 4 or below in her eyes, you ain't got a chance. Move on. Since I coach men from all over the world for a living, most guys spend way too much time interacting with or being hung up on women who have little to no romantic attraction for them. The average guy, since he does not know what he's doing and how attraction works, is literally talking women right out of sleeping with him. If you frequent bars and nightclubs… watch, observe and listen. You will see a woman be excited to talk to a guy, but within a few minutes she's trying to get away and he has no idea! You can verify everything I teach by watching men and women interact. It's fascinating to people watch.

I looked right at her and asked her to dinner the next night, with a specific time and place. She will tell you that my presence and confidence left her no choice but to accept. She said, "I couldn't say no." She told me that no one had ever asked her out by being so direct and sure of himself. She also told me later that guys had been coming up to her all week, with the: *Hey, would you like to get dinner or lunch and get to know each other* type of line. But the way they went about it said immediately that they were weak and had no confidence. They weren't direct and they gave no specifics, leaving it wide open. I just said: *Let's go to dinner, at this time, at this place*, and she went along with it. Definite dates are the subtle difference that makes all the difference when it comes to setting dates women actually keep.

We met the next night after the event was over and never did order dinner. We ended up having tea all night. We were talking so much, or I should say, *she* was talking so much. I let her do about 80% of the talking and I just kept asking her questions. That by the way, is how to remain mysterious and cause a woman to be even more curious about you and romantically interested in you by the end of your date. I was totally fascinated by her. At about three o'clock in the morning when the cleaning crew started cleaning the carpet; we finally felt it was time to go. As we stood up to leave, I couldn't help myself. I reached across the table and started kissing her. Then I walked her back to her hotel down the street.

The rest of the week we were always with each other, as though we had been together for years. Even others who saw us thought we had been together for years. It was so effortless. There was no holding back. We were holding hands and we were affectionate. I had no doubt of myself, I showed no fear, and I showed zero lack of confidence because of the little known secrets I had mastered. Because of the presence that I exuded, she hardly tested me at all.

We spent months at a time together over the next year. We explored various places – Paris, London, Orlando, Miami, Colorado, sharing new discoveries around us and in each other. We had a lot of similar interests, and she was into personal growth and development.

We communicated, which is a major point in relationships. Google "Corey Wayne How To Communicate With Women Effectively." I always knew where she was at and how she felt toward me. I knew how to continually read her attraction level and how to see signs when I was becoming too complacent in the relationship.

Eventually we ended up going our separate ways. Neither of us was ready to make a commitment to marriage, and she went back to school in the U.K. I couldn't go from seeing her for several months at a time to seeing her for ten days every three months. I needed more than that. When we did end the relationship, it was hard. It was hardest because we both truly loved each other – and we still do.

Our whole time together while dating was effortless. We never fought or argued. We were always affectionate, loving, kind, and focused on giving to one another. We never focused on what we were getting from each other, or were jealous or needy. It was all about loving each other unconditionally and never being judgmental. Even when we decided to end our intimate relationship and see other people, we did it with love.

If two people truly love each other and want to be happy with their choice to go their separate ways, I do not think it is the loving thing to do to cut one another off from all communication. I actually think that makes it harder to heal. The hard part about a relationship ending is the finality of it all. Going from being each others' best friend and lover to no longer speaking is not being loving in my opinion. It just seeks to hurt the other person. Many people feel that trying to hurt the other person will make them feel better.

I think sharing your feelings with each other when a relationship ends is very helpful and important to the healing process. The purpose of an intimate relationship, in my opinion, is to love each other and to help each other grow and become more. You're there to meet each others' needs. The whole purpose of a relationship is you go there to give. The only thing we lost when our relationship ended was the physical intimacy.

Any relationship is about giving. It is not about what you get. We decided we wanted to give a little differently than we did before. By loving each other through the transition, there was no need to hurt or feel a loss. The things that make a relationship hurt when it ends is the loss of all contact with the person we love. We built on what we had created in our year together, and therefore there was nothing to lose. We still talk via email a few times a year and she's now a Chiropractor, living in Finland.

Once guys really understand women and are able to get into a relationship, they will eventually realize, like I did, that every relationship is an opportunity for growth. Just because you absolutely adore and treasure the person you're with, it doesn't mean that you will spend the rest of your life with that person, or even marry them.

I read once that only 3% or 3 out of 100 men understand women. In my experience, this is an accurate figure. If you want relationship heartaches to be over and to become one of the 3% of men that understand women, then read and apply the principles that are here. Then go back and read them again to retain the knowledge. When you think you have it down pat, read it again.

These are principles that I have learned from numerous sources and applied in my own life. I know they work and in the following pages you will find the truth to finally understanding women. I will not only give you simple "how to" examples, but I will explain why things are the way they are from an emotional, spiritual, physical, and mental point of view.

The purpose of my life is to help others grow and become more. I don't want anyone to have to grow up in a loveless family like I did. It sucks. I did not enjoy my childhood very much. By understanding this, you can at least be in a relationship with someone that you absolutely love, treasure, and adore. I can teach you how to have a great relationship and keep the perfect girl attracted long term, but I can't make you stay in love with them. They can help you to understand the type of man that you are totally capable of becoming and even become that man. At the same time, you inspire and help her grow into everything she is capable of becoming as a woman. If the relationship reaches a point where it is no longer an opportunity for both people to continue growing together, then it's time to move on. "When you meet someone whose soul isn't aligned with yours... send them love and move on." ~ Dr. Wayne Dyer.

I have done all the hard work and spent many years of heartache and heartbreak to learn and understand this knowledge. I've been successfully applying the best self-help principles over the past two and a half decades. I teach what works, not theory. If you choose to have faith and apply what you learn here, you will become attuned and will be able to read exactly what is going on with your lady emotionally at every moment and completely understand what she needs. It will put you in the driver's seat in your intimate relationships. "Excellence is not a singular act but a habit. You are what you do repeatedly." ~ Aristotle.

You will be able to help your friends and family overcome their relationship struggles as well. However, I have found that very few people actually are open to learning new relationship skills. While you are learning this information and applying it, do not seek the advice of your friends unless you are 100% certain they understand women. It is very simple – unless they have the kind of relationship you wish to create in your own life, don't ask them for advice.

Enjoy the knowledge that appears in the following pages and I want you to know I have immense love, respect, and care for you and your desire to have the relationship of your dreams. I was once searching like you are now. I wanted to find the answer. I found a lot of answers from a lot of different sources and have put down in these pages the best of the information that I personally use.

It is important for you to understand that you should not read this book and then go out and settle down with the first woman you meet. This book is about finding the type of woman you feel you deserve to be with. Those feelings may change and evolve over time, as you change and evolve as a person. You may find the absolute perfect woman for you on day one, and then six months later realize that there are subtle differences you would make that would create an even better situation for you. It's about constantly refining your criteria, and in the meantime, having the experiences you need in order to learn, so you can eventually focus 100% on the woman of your dreams. Google "Corey Wayne How To Attract The Perfect Woman." You won't have to spend your time with her wondering if the grass is greener on the other side of the fence. You will have been on the other side and experienced it. I want you to have someone who knocks your socks off! Besides, that is your birthright as a child of the Creator.

I will focus on giving you tools for lasting change so you can permanently undo your not-so-desirable habits and bring out the amazing man you are inside – the one that all women are just dying to meet. The great news is that you already have this natural talent and ability inside. If you will allow me to coach you how to be comfortable being yourself, then you can be a 3% man and you will own the heart of your lady for life.

Part II: The Way Things Are

My Evolution of Understanding

I have dated many beautiful women. In my earlier years I said and did all the wrong things that we men tend to do. In my later years of dating, I finally got it right. So how did I go from clueless wonder to this point of understanding? There was one woman, my missing link, if you will, that opened my eyes to understanding women. Don't get me wrong, *all* the women in my life, and *all* of my dating experiences helped bring me to the point where I am today. But it was this particular woman that helped me put it all together.

I mentioned this story in the introduction, but I wanted to go over it again to show how this particular relationship actually helped to evolve my understanding of women. In my earlier years of dating, somewhere around 1994, I met this woman. She had dark hair, dark eyes, nice skin, and she was tiny. She told me straight out: *I'm 105 pounds*. We had gone to high school together, but she had been a year behind me. I hadn't seen her for a couple years and I was out with a good friend of mine. She walked up and I was just stunned. Her beauty left me breathless.

I was having some beers with my buddy Sean and he introduced us. I could tell she was interested by the way she was looking at me. I could *feel* that she was really attracted to me. That was my first awareness of understanding. There had been several times in my life where I had *thought* a woman was attracted to me, and then could never get any further than her phone number. This was blatant and in my face. I could FEEL her attraction. There was no doubt in my mind that this woman had a high level of attraction.

I was still pretty clueless back then, though. The night went on and we went our separate ways. When I woke up the next day, the horrible feeling dawned on me: I didn't get her number. However, she had told me where she worked. I took a chance and called her at work and basically said: *Hi, this is Corey*. She told me she was really busy, but asked me to give her my number and she would call me back the next day. Deep down I feared she would never call back like all the others.

I gave her my number and I was just so in awe. I actually had butterflies in my stomach. This was the first time I had met a girl that I really liked that was also really into me. She actually called me the next day and I talked to her for at least an hour and a half on the phone. While we talked, she told me things such as she had just split up with her boyfriend, and then went on to volunteer all this other information about herself. She was asking me all these questions like: *How come you don't have a girlfriend?*

I was kind of an open book. I wasn't very mysterious. It wasn't until later that I figured out I hadn't handled that part the right way. The right thing to do would have been to talk for no more than 10 minutes and then say, *"Hey, when are you free to meet up for a drink?"* make definite plans and get off the phone. However, she did most of the talking, which was exactly the right thing to do. Honestly, I don't really remember much of what I said to her. I just let her talk and I listened. I have found that women love to talk, men just need to learn *how* to listen.

Believe me, gentlemen, there is a right and wrong way to the art of listening that we will be covering later in the book. Finally she asked: *Why don't we go to lunch this week?* I jumped right on that and set a date. That was another thing I did right without even realizing it: I made a firm commitment for a date, and then left it at that.

So, she showed up for lunch that day wearing these really short shorts. She had an unbelievable body with a nice tan, and she was breathtaking – absolutely drop dead gorgeous. I was working construction at the time. I was still going to school for construction management and I was a project engineer at the job site office. I was in the back and I heard the door open and she walked in. The guys called out from the front, saying: *Corey, your lunch date's here.* When I walked out, the guys had been having a meeting at the conference table and they were just staring at her. It felt so good, because she was obviously there to go out with me.

That was another thing I did right. I **knew** she was there for me and took pride in it. It didn't make me jealous to have all these guys staring at the woman I was dating. They were jealous of me being with her, but they were enjoying what they were seeing. In that regard, I was in a place of strength and confidence. A woman definitely takes notice of little things like that.

We went up the street and had a great lunch. Again, she did most of the talking, which was the right thing. The truth is that I was nervous and couldn't think of much to say, so she just went on talking. She was very aggressive. After that first date, she was paging me and we'd meet out and have some drinks. With hindsight, I realize now that she was pursuing me because I did so little of the talking. I was a bit of a mystery to her. In reality, I was an open book and not sure enough of myself to speak up. She just had not caught onto that yet. My only thought was: *This is great. This girl's all over me.*

Her dad was very wealthy and he owned a night club in Fort Lauderdale. One night she invited me there. I went with another friend of mine. It was a very busy club. She had all these guys coming up to her and hugging her, and she seemed to know everybody there. She kept walking away and talking, and all these people kept grabbing her to talk. Finally, my friend said: *Let's go, dude. She doesn't care about you.*

I was pretty bummed out, but agreed. She really didn't seem to care whether I was there or not. The next morning she called me and asked: *What happened to you last night? I looked everywhere for you.* I held the phone away, thinking: *What?* I found out by accident that I had done the right thing, and I had just walked away. "The strongest negotiating position is being able to walk away and mean it." ~ Michael Yon. What is the quickest way to gain someone's attention? Remove yours.

If a woman is too sure of you, if she thinks she can walk all over you, her attraction drops. As I said earlier, it's a scientific fact that women are more attracted to men whose feelings are unclear. Most of the time women won't call you and ask you out. They'll simply call to say, "I had a great time the other night. I was thinking about you. Hey, this is really random..." and then proceed to talk about some innocuous subject. Think of dating like playing poker. You simply want to hold your cards close to your vest so she reveals her cards first. When women are uncertain or unclear of your interest, they will put themselves into your orbit by contacting you. When a woman starts chasing you by initiating contact first (usually after the 2nd or 3rd date on average), it causes her to start chasing you more and more. She'll call, text, email, message, etc. more and more as the weeks go by. It's always better if a woman thinks that she wants you a little more than you want her. When that happens, talk for only a few minutes and then ask, "Hey when are you free to get together again?" and make your next date. You should always assume that when a woman reaches out to you, she's really trying to make it easy for you to make another date to get together. Once a woman feels comfortable enough, she will start calling you more and more as the weeks go by, assuming you keep doing more things right than wrong. So by not sitting back and letting her walk all over me, by walking away, I demonstrated my strength in letting her know that I wasn't going to take being ignored. I showed that I could walk away from her at any time. That wasn't the truth of what had happened, but that wasn't how she saw it.

I had walked away because I felt she didn't care about me and now she wanted to know where I was at and what I was doing. It baffled me at the time. This went on for another two or three weeks and we went out a couple more times. I never did kiss her. We hugged every time we saw each other, but I just didn't have the guts to go for it.

How do you know when a woman is open to being kissed? As you are talking and you are sitting close, her knee may be touching yours, she may be touching your arm or body, she may be leaning toward you, standing so close that her body is bumping yours, etc., then as she's talking slowly, move your eyes from looking into hers to looking at her lips, then back to her eyes, slowly back to her lips and then into her eyes again over the course of 5-7 seconds. If she looks at your lips at any time while you are doing this, it means she's ready to be kissed.

Do it! If you wait and hesitate too long, she will lose attraction and assume you are not worthy.

Eventually, she stopped calling. It got to the point where I called her and left her a message. She called me the next day at my house, but she knew I wasn't there. I was at work. She had always paged me before. So she had called me at home on purpose, when she knew I wouldn't be there.

The bottom line was that I was so easy and so available, that she saw me as weak and thought she could basically have her way with me. She would invite me to come out and I would meet her. I didn't take control. I had no center. Eventually she saw that and then she just blew me off. A guy who is good looking can get away on his looks for the first few dates. If he's not centered, weak, and always does what she wants, her attraction will lower to the point where she doesn't want to see him any more. That was what happened with me. I was devastated.

It was about six months later when I met the woman who would become my ex-wife. I remember being out on a date at the same bar where I had met the other woman. My ex-wife was all over me, and I remember seeing the other woman out of the corner of my eye, just staring at the two of us together. Once again, I was confused, thinking: *I don't get it. I'm with somebody else. She didn't want me before. Now I'm with my new girlfriend and she's always checking me out.* If I was out without my ex-wife, she'd come up and flirt with me. I kept thinking: *What gives? I don't get it.* Women like a guy who has options with women, but don't rub it directly in her face. When you are with a woman and she knows or assumes you are dating other women, just make her feel a little more special than the other girls you are dating. Otherwise, she'll assume you plan on having sex and blowing her off as another notch in your bedpost. So if she says, "how many other women are you dating?" say, "I don't kiss and tell, but none of those girls are as awesome as you are, honey." with a James Bond smirk on your face. That's all. Keep it simple, charming, playful and little vague. Let her fill in the blanks in her mind.

It is all about the energy and the confidence the guy exudes. I'm sure every guy has had this experience – whenever they are dating someone, every girl wants them. When they are single, no one wants to date them. Women have this radar. When a woman sees a guy with a woman, especially another beautiful woman, she wonders: *Hmmm…what's that guy got?* Women are very competitive in that respect.

Why You Should Not Get Advice From Women about Women

When I was having trouble understanding women, I remember going to my women friends for advice. I figured: *Hey, they're women, so they should have a clue and be able to help me out, right?* Wrong. The advice they gave me *seemed* sound, and it meshed with what I had always thought about women. This sometimes pisses women off, but the truth is, the average woman does not understand what attracts them to one guy vs. another. What they say they want in a man is not what they actually date and stay with.

Most women, when you bring your problems about understanding another woman to them, will try to make you feel better about what is going on. It is just like when you try to date a woman, she is not going to tell you straight out: *Hey, I'm really not interested.* A woman friend is not going to burst your ego and tell you: *Hey, it sounds as though she just doesn't like you. Move on.* Instead, they will give you rationalizations: *Maybe she is just coming out of a bad relationship. Maybe she really isn't getting your calls. Maybe she just likes you too much and is afraid of getting into something right now.* Women are emotional beings and will always think about how what they say is going to make you feel. So take their advice with a grain of salt.

Why do women, even our female friends, do this to us? I believe it is mostly because they don't want to deal with your questions of: *So tell me why she doesn't like me. Is there something wrong with me?* without hurting your feelings. They would rather try to soothe it over and nudge you gently in another direction, rather than being straight up about their suspicions and hurt you.

Women are all about emotions and emotional reactions. Men are more straightforward. While men may deal from a place of emotions, they don't take time to necessarily look at the emotional side of the equation. They would rather have simple, non-emotionally clouded answers. The trouble is that our women friends do nothing more than cloud the issue rather than setting us straight.

Why Women Want to Chase You

Another part of it is that women often know what they want; they just don't know how to express it in terms of how to get there. Women *say* they want romance, and on a certain level that's true. But they also want to be engaged in the chase. Dating is a full experience of emotions for them. They don't want everything dropped in their laps. They want to feel as though they have earned your love, and that you have earned theirs.

Here's how to get women to chase you by understanding the love and relationship dynamic between little girls and their fathers. Little girls tend to go to their fathers and sit in their laps for love and reassurance. When a girl becomes unsure of herself, afraid or upset, she will go sit in her daddy's lap for love and reassurance. He is her rock. Her unmovable Mountain that is always there and always accepts and loves her unconditionally. He makes her feel safe and comfortable.

I remember a trip to the beach I took one time with a former girlfriend, her 7-year-old daughter and some family. During the day we were in the pool because it was hot. The father of my girlfriend's daughter was never around very much. He was constantly disappointing her. I remember the sad look on her face after her father would tell her he was not going to be seeing her when she wanted to see him. It made her feel like he did not love her. However, I was the father figure that took his place when he was not around, which was most of the time. As I was standing in the middle of the pool, my girlfriend's daughter kept jumping from the side of the pool into my arms. It was more like she would fall into my arms so I would grab her and embrace her. She got in and out of the pool dozens of times to do this. She never tired of it.

I remember another time when I was picking up her daughter to take her for the day to Disney World, one of her favorite places. As I was driving to pick her up, she would call me to see where I was and how close I was. When I arrived at her grandmother's house to pick her up, she said to me with a big beautiful smile on her face, "Stop! Wait there!" So I stopped as she started to run toward me. She jumped into my arms as I knelt down to catch her. I picked her up for a big hug and kiss. I loved that little munchkin, and still do today even though she's all grown up! Time flies! She totally opened my heart and changed my life. Kids are our greatest teachers.

The important thing to understand about the love and relationship dynamic between little girls and their fathers and why it causes women to chase the men they desire, is they both crave the unconditional love and masculine presence of the men they love or care about. When a woman contacts you by telephone, text, e-mail, instant message, etc., she is looking for you to communicate through your actions that she is loved, wanted and adored. When women become unsure of where they stand with you or when they miss you, they contact you so you can make it easy for them to get the love and reassurance they are seeking. So if a woman contacts you, you must assume it is because she wants you physically, emotionally, spiritually and mentally. She wants to be penetrated by you and your love. Obviously, little girls grow up and have adult relationships with the men they love. However, the dynamic of how women go about getting this love is similar to how they seek love and support from their fathers.

When a woman contacts you, she wants you in some way. If you really love and care about her, you will facilitate getting together. Women assume that if you do not facilitate getting together when they contact you, that you don't care for them or want them. It does not matter what you say, what you promise in the future or what you did for them last week. If you don't make a date or make room in your schedule for her right now, she will assume that you don't love her that much anymore. When women do not feel that you love them, or love them enough, they will feel hurt and often become bitchy and resentful. Google "Corey Wayne Men: Beware Of The Bitchy Woman."

Think about what this means. Women will chase you if you give them the space to miss you by not chasing them. Your inaction will cause them to take some action to get confirmation that you care and desire them. In essence, all you really have to do is simply say yes to their advances. If a woman is chasing you, she can't be getting rid of you. Why chase women when women not only are dying to chase you, but they've been training, conditioning, thinking, feeling and acting as the pursuer of masculine love & presence their whole lives? Men who chase women get rejected because the very act of chasing a woman is a submissive feminine quality. Plus, it simply will not feel right to a woman if you chase her. If you do she will become flakey, unsure of things, confused, etc.

One of the biggest booming industries in the publishing world that caters to women is the romance novel. They sell millions of these books to women all over the world. You will find that even the most intelligent of women, ones that proclaim these books to be nothing more than drivel, have read one or two of these books at one time or another in their lives. What is the big draw?

Most of your romance novels have a very basic formula to them. You can even go to the manuscript submission pages for the publishing houses and find what that formula is: Boy meets girl. Boy usually treats girl with indifference. Girl finds boy contemptible, yet cannot seem to stay away from him. Girl and boy fight the growing attraction. Boy ends up with girl in a very romantic ending.

When you ask a woman what she wants, what she *says* she wants and what she actually emotionally responds to are two different things. When you ask a woman what she wants in a guy, she will usually respond with something like: *Well, I want a man that wines me, dines me, and buys me flowers.* When you treat her that way, she blows you off and for some reason goes out with a guy who does none of those things for her. Everybody has seen the guy that's dating a beautiful woman and is kind of a jerk to her. So what is it that attracts her to the bad boy and causes her to blow off the nice guy? Google "Corey Wayne Women Want A Man Who Is A Challenge."

The simple answer to that is the nice guy is easy. She can completely have her way with him. He's not strong. He's not centered. He acts more like a woman than a man. Emotionally, that does not make her feel safe or that he could actually protect her. It says to her that he is untrustworthy, and that basically he will do or say anything just to make her happy. She won't trust his masculine core because if he won't stand up for himself to her, and if she were ever in any physical danger, he'd bolt and leave her to defend herself. That is not what a woman wants. A woman wants someone who is a partner, someone who can take the direction in the relationship. An alpha male is a leader. A man's job is to lead the interaction to where HE WANTS it to go. Whether you have just met, or you have been together in a 10-year relationship, you have to know what you want.

It's like when you call a woman you have just met and you ask her out. Instead of saying: *Well, gee, do you think maybe you'd like to go out with me sometime?* Basically, what that tells a woman is: *I'm not really confident and I really don't think I'm good enough for you, but I'm hoping that maybe you'll have pity on me and grace me with your presence on a date.*

The more beautiful a woman is – the more guys she has that act that way. She wants a guy that is going to stand out. She wants him to be more of a man than she is. The more beautiful woman she is, the more choices that she has. If she goes out on an average weekend, she might give her phone number out to 10 or 12 different guys. Predictably, what happens is that 9 or 10 of those guys are going to call her the very next day and ask her to go out on a date. From that point, she can basically decide which ones she wants to go out with, or if she wants to go out with any of them at all.

Your goal is to be different. You do not want to give a woman the impression that you haven't had a date in 10 years, even if that is the case. There are some simple, subtle things that you need to learn about raising her attraction level, approaching her properly, asking for her number and setting definite dates with confidence.

Most guys, even if they do manage to get the phone number of a woman that they are interested in, can't seem to manage to get to her front porch or meet up for that all important first date. If they do go out on a date, they can't seem to ever get another one with the same woman. On the other hand, the girls that they don't really have much interest in are calling and chasing them. They are pursuing them, and really want to be with them. The simple answer is that you basically have to treat the ones you *do* like just like the ones you *don't* like. Of course, there's a lot more to it than that, but it's a start. I will be going into that more in depth later in the book.

One of the other things that we will cover is once you are dating and starting to get serious about a woman, what to do to maintain her level of attraction. Most guys think that once they're going steady with their girlfriend, or once they get married, the "courtship is over". They get this complacent attitude of: *Oh, wow, now I've got this relationship thing handled. I can just kick back and drink my beers and just sit in front of the TV all weekend and eat chips and pizza. I'm set.*

That is not the case. The courtship continues. It will be on-going your entire life. It never ends. Many guys find it easy to get a girl and have her fall in love, but they are not able to maintain that level of love, and don't understand why. A lot of guys have had their girlfriend just up and leave them, or their wife has just up and left them after 10 years, and they say: *What the hell happened? I thought everything was great. I thought things were perfect, and now all of the sudden, she's gone.* They don't have any idea what happened.

Why You Should Never Listen To Your Friends about Dating Advice

One of the reasons it's hard to get good advice, even from your friends, is that there are very few people that actually have healthy, loving relationships. Even the guys that really understand women can't seem to tell you specifically what you have to do. They just own their masculinity, they own their strength, and they own their core, purpose, and direction in life. They are naturally confident with women, because they grew up in a very loving household, or they have learned for themselves what it takes.

I have a few close friends who are naturally good with women. One of them is one of my best friends from high school. I've learned a ton about women from him over the years. He's been with his wife almost 20 years. They have three beautiful children together. He was a stud in high school, college and back when we were single and hunting in our early 20's he did really well. His wife looks hot and still takes care of herself. She still looks like she's in her 20's even though she's in her 40's now. They've had maybe 7 or 8 fights total over the last 20 years they've been together. Their attitude is... why fight? We're in this together. It's about meeting each other's needs and enjoying each other. They both came from good loving families so things were easy for them.

Another friend of mine is in his 70's now. He's been with his wife over 4 decades! He is so charming and awesome at charming banter. They still have a great sex life. He was a well-known musician back in the 1970's and early 1980's. He did the same thing with his first wife that I did with my first wife. He settled. He got married at 21 and right when he was about to tell her he was leaving her a few months later because he made a mistake, she revealed she was pregnant. Twelve years and two kids later he finally got the courage to leave. His current wife of 40 plus years was only 18 when they met. He was 33. They had two kids and are now grandparents. He taught me a lot about women! His wife loves the shit out of him.

When you come to your friends to talk about a woman and what is going on in your relationship, their first instinct is to give you advice. But should you listen to your friends' advice about women? Ask yourself this question first: *What kind of a relationship does my friend have?* Use the same radar that you will learn from what I teach you to gauge his woman's attraction level in him. Does she seem happy in the relationship? Is she loving and affectionate to him? Is he ignoring her while she goes about and does her own thing? What *is* her interest level in your friend?

If you look at your friends' relationships, do you see what you want your relationship to become? If the answer is yes, then maybe your friends have a clue. If the answer is no, as it usually will be, then why on earth would you want to take their advice for your own relationship? Face the facts. If they do not have relationships that you want to emulate, all their good intentions in the world won't lead you to the relationship you truly deserve to have in your life.

How Many Healthy Relationships Do You See Out There?

The number of healthy relationships out there, while increasing due to some of the awareness being brought to the concept, is still pretty low. Why is that? I once believed I had great parents. In retrospect, I realize that there was no real love shown between them. There was never an: *I love you* exchanged that I ever witnessed. Why should that be such a big deal?

When there is no love shown between the parents, it creates insecurity in their children. In my case, when I went out into the dating world, I was shy and insecure. I didn't feel as though I had anything to offer. I felt unloved and unlovable. When children grow up around parents that do not show love to each other, children in turn perpetuate that in their own relationships in the future. Is that the type of relationship that you want for your children? The same kind of loveless, trapped relationship you may be in now? One you may have been exposed to by your own parents?

Parents stay together for years without showing the proper example of a loving, healthy relationship to their children. This in turn makes kids think: *That's just the way things are.* They become emotionally and mentally conditioned and anchored into feeling like dysfunctional relationships are normal. If the parents had worked to maintain a healthy relationship, or separated into other, healthier relationships, the kids might have had a clue by the time they reached their own teenage dating years.

I had one friend who was married to a girl that he got pregnant at the age of 16 or 17. Over the years, what may have seemed like love at first, turned into a marriage solely for the sake of the children. He began to have an affair. She started gaining weight – a lot of weight. She was seeking her happiness in food and using it to fill her up with that *feel good* sensation she was missing in her marriage.

At a wedding for a mutual friend, both the husband and wife shot one negative barb after another at each other. Both of their boys were extremely obese, very unhappy, and had very low self-esteem. These children hadn't even reached dating age and they were already caught in the same trap of misery perpetuated by their parents. They will probably end up seeking out the same type of relationships for themselves, never knowing that there can be better for them. They will end up perpetuating the pain for another generation.

Parents may think they are staying together for the sake of the children, but kids need to see parents in happy, loving, supportive relationships. The choices you make in your relationship life can certainly have an impact on the other people around you, especially the kids. There is also the impact on yourself to consider, as well as the happiness of the other person in the relationship. I have already said it before - if you are not growing together in a direction, then maybe you need to consider going your separate ways so that you can continue to grow. The quality of your life is in direct proportion to the quality of the people you consistently spend your time with. That's something to think about!

The ultimate impact in a relationship that involves children is how they carry their own relationship knowledge forward with them, into the next generation. Your legacy to your children should be learning what unconditional love looks like, not only in your love for them, but in your love for your partner. *Your* example is what sets the way for them to find the same kind of love in their lives in the future. Ultimately, the only way to see healthier relationships around us is to be a part of building our own happiness and letting it follow forward through the next generation.

Perceptions of Control

It is so important that people learn the information I have to offer. Again, only 3% of all men actually understand women. The divorce rate is over 50%, and the other 47% are simply too weak or not miserable enough to do anything about it. All you have to do is go to a mall, to a public event, or to dinner, and just look around at the other couples. Half of them are sort of staring into space, and they are not talking. I've gone to dinner and seen couples where the husband is reading a magazine and the wife is reading the paper. They are just kind of present. They are hanging out as roommates. They probably haven't had sex in years either. There is nothing *there* in the relationship.

A man should learn to take the direction in the relationship. It is funny when you go to the malls, and you can tell who wears the pants in the relationship. You usually see the woman walking about 5, sometimes 10 feet in front of the man and the kids. The husband is walking as though being led by the nose, going along with whatever she wants. She is in total control of the relationship.

If you are with your lady, you should either be holding her hand or walking side by side with her as a true equal. The bottom line is that the one in charge of the relationship, the one that's in control, is the one that is always in front. You can hear them talking as they go along: *What do you want to do, honey? Oh, I don't know, honey, what do you want to do?* Women don't want control! They want the man to make the decisions and make the plans. Women just want to show up for a date looking hot, have fun and have the man lead things successfully into the bedroom.

I used to go out with a woman, she's 29 now, and always dates guys that are in their 40's or 50's. These guys are the biggest pushovers in their relationships with her. They take her flying on their corporate jet and throw tons of money at her. I used to tease her about her engagement ring collection, because she had four or five guys that had bought her engagement rings.

Masculine and Feminine Energy

The problem is that she is so in her masculine side. We would go out, and I'd have to spend over an hour working on getting her to be playful, to be a girl. She would start out: *Oh turn left on this road and go this way.* I would have to say: *I know where I'm going, just relax. Just be a girl and have fun. I have everything handled. Just have a good time tonight. Don't worry about it. I am not like the regular guys you go out with.*

Her father is a great guy, but he's very weak and her mother runs the household. So she learned to run the household and the relationship from her mother. She is always in her masculine side, and yet she is drop dead gorgeous. She competed for Miss America, has a perfect body, her Masters degree and a contractor's license. She is very successful, has her own business and her own TV show. Most guys are intimidated by her looks because she's so beautiful. In addition to that, she is *so* strong – she is *so* in her masculine side – that the only kinds of guys she can get are very feminine guys.

A guy needs to make his mind up about what it is he wants to do. Women don't want to have to make all the decisions. That's why, if you have been in a relationship for a long time and say: *Hey honey, what do you want to do tonight?* She'll throw it back into your lap: *What do you want to do?* You: *I don't know honey, what do you want to do?* In other words, women are saying: *Will you make a decision, already? For crying out loud!*

That is a masculine strength quality. A guy that's direct, has a purpose in life, and says: *Hey honey, let's go to the movies tonight,* will likely get a: *Great! Let's go to the movies.* You have to be the one that sets the plans and knows what you are doing. Women just want to be able to go out, relax, completely get in their feminine side, and just let the guy take total control. All a guy really needs to focus on when dating is hangout, have fun and hook up. Hangout: make a definite date in the evening that can potentially lead to you having sex at her place or yours later in the evening. Have fun: keep things funny and positive with no complicated situations or subjects; just do something fun. Hook up: go for the kiss. Kissing leads to heavy petting, which leads to you saying something like, "hey, let's get out of here, grab a bottle of wine and go back to my place." Seduction is the process of getting closer and closer to her until you end up inside of her.

Once you are past the first few months and your lady is totally in love with you, at that point, the more of your presence and love that you give your lady, the more she wants from you. Women are about opening up and receiving your love and your presence. That is the feminine energy. The masculine energy is all about purpose, drive, direction, and mission in life. The masculine energy is also about breaking through barriers.

Between men and women, the woman opens up and receives. She is physically designed to receive a man. She is penetrated in every way by her man: emotionally, mentally, spiritually and physically. And a man in every way penetrates the world and his woman. So the more you give to your lady, the more she wants from you. By only calling/texting her once a week for one date in the beginning per week, you create the conditions for her to start calling and texting you more and more. After the 2nd or 3rd date when she starts contacting you first because she does not want to wait until next week to hear from you again, you'll then start seeing each other about twice per week. By the 5th or 6th week you'll be seeing her 3-4 times per week. By week 7 and 8 she will be calling/texting/messaging you 2-3 times per day and pretty much be with you all the time. By sticking to once per week only where you initiate contact, she'll reach out more and more as her attraction grows. Then, all you have to do is make your next date when she calls. By the end of two months she'll be bringing up being exclusive because she's falling in love. Hangout, have fun and hook up. Rinse. Recycle. Repeat.

That's why a woman will call you during the day: *Hey, I'm just calling to see what you're doing.* It is a big billboard that says: *Hey, I want to feel your love. I want to feel your presence.* That's why when you walk in the door, she doesn't have to tell you she loves you. She runs up to you and wraps her arms around you and kisses you. It is because she wants to feel the love that you have for her. That's why when she says: *Hey, look, I got my nails done today.* And you say:

Honey, I'm watching TV. It is one of the worst things you can do. You are basically saying to her: *I don't love you. I'm not giving you any of my presence. Get the hell out of my way. You are unimportant to me right now.* You are invalidating what is important to her, and leaving her feeling unloved. Bad move.

When she says: *I just got my hair done, what do you think, honey?* You have to stop what you are doing, and say: *You look beautiful. You look great... she did a great job. I love your nails... I love that new dress you just bought. Your new hair color looks great. That new handbag? I think it goes great with that outfit. You look really hot.*

Women want to be noticed. Everything they do is about getting your attention. That's why it is so important to understand this. One of my most recent testimonials was from a friend who told me I saved his relationship. His girlfriend was doing everything she could to try and get his attention. All she wanted to do was *feel* him. I told him: *Your sole purpose for being in that relationship is to give to her. So you either need to give to her, or go out and get yourself a hooker. That way you can have a transactional based relationship with no emotional attachments.* Once he understood that, he realized everything she was doing – the clothes she was wearing, the hair – it was all about her saying: *I want to feel your love. I want to feel your presence.*

When a woman stops doing those things, she has basically closed herself off from you. She has shut down, and now you will have a lot of work to do before you can get through and penetrate those barriers. She has put this wall up. **You** have shut her down because you haven't given her your presence. It is now going to be ten times as difficult for you to get back into her heart again. She is going to test you and make it really hard, because she wants to make sure that if she ***does*** open up to receive your love that you are going to ***give*** that love and presence to her. That's why communication is so important.

I'm not going to tell you that having a healthy, loving relationship is easy. It takes a lot of work. However, I can tell you from experience that if you take the time to understand your woman, she will help you to make that healthy, loving relationship effortless. Again, it is all about knowing who you are, knowing what you want, being in your center, and understanding your woman. Once you get these concepts, you can not only have a wonderful, loving relationship, but you can grow in your own person, help her to grow in her own person, and perpetuate a healthy, loving lifestyle that will be emulated for generations to come.

Part III: The Art of Understanding

Looking for Love

We are all trying to get love or give love in everything we do. It is a natural part of human nature. How we look for love, and what kind of love it is that we look for can depend on how we were raised. It can also depend on what we have come to understand about ourselves and the things that become important to us in our lives. Have we learned from past mistakes and evolved to a new level of understanding? Or do we go forward in the manner of the true crazy person that continues to repeat the same actions over and over again and expects different results?

Women and men look for love in different ways. Many guys, by the second or third date are saying: *I love you.* Women are responding with reservation, either inwardly or outwardly saying: *What? You don't even know me yet.* Thich Nhat Hanh says that, "You must love in such a way that the person you love feels free." When a guy starts professing his love after only a few dates and starts putting out the relationship vibe, it's simply inappropriate and out of sequence. Women are emotional beings and they get scared when a guy tries to get too serious too soon by focusing on relationship labels or locking them down to a commitment. Commitment, bonding and being together 24/7 happens slowly over several months as the woman's level of attraction for you grows. When she's ready for a relationship or a commitment, she'll bring it up. If she's not bringing it up, it means she's not at that point yet. Simply continue to focus on hanging out, having fun and hooking up when you are together. Slowly over time she won't want to be with anyone else other that you. If you try to force or rush the process, she will reject you.

Guys are physical, for the most part. They are very visual. A guy is going to look at a woman and know instantly whether he is interested or not. He is going to look at her hair, her eyes, her body, and instantly have a high level of sexual attraction for her, or not. Even though a guy has not spoken to a woman, or before he knows anything about her, he instantly tends to size her up. If a guy meets a woman, is talking to her, and thinks she is very beautiful, many times he will look past a lot of other qualities that he may not like, just because he is visually stimulated.

A guy will have an instant reaction to a woman and say things like: *Oh, wow. I'm going to marry her.* Guys connect physically and in an instant can engage their emotions. Women take longer. They warm up more slowly to a reaction of interest. A woman needs to understand who the guy is before she will enter into that emotional reaction, and often before she will engage physically. Women go out of first dates with the attitude of just seeing what happens. The guy tends to be focused on making her his girlfriend and possessing her instead of just letting the love story develop.

To a woman, when a guy is engaging his emotions at the beginning of the relationship, without taking the time to get to know who she is first, he seems needy. Because of the way women deal with emotions and love, they can't quite comprehend the man's instantaneous emotional response. It makes her leery and uncomfortable. She doesn't feel safe with him, because he is not in his masculine. Guys who are needy tend to act like creepy stalkers. All women have met guys like this in the past and most know how to spot the control freaks, stalkers and needy guys.

At that point, she is not seeing him as a strong, centered man. A woman that has a strong feminine core will be completely turned off by a man that is acting outside the strong masculine area where he should be. She might not even necessarily know **what** it is about him that is turning her off, but she will rapidly lose any attraction that might have been there from her first assessment.

Don't Be So Serious

You don't have to declare your love to a woman for her to know that you are interested. In fact, the chances are higher that you will turn her off immediately. A woman **knows** when you're interested in her. Women intuitively know these simple things. It is common sense to them, but not to us guys.

Women understand men far better than men understand women. She knows when a guy is interested, because she has taken time to develop this sense. Guys don't have that advantage. They don't know what to look for, and will often project their own attraction level on to the woman, totally clueless of where she is really at. The whole process that I will be taking you through in this book helps a man to develop the same sense of awareness a woman has. So you give a woman the space to fall for you and come to you at her own pace to the point that she thinks it's her idea.

When a guy meets a woman, he will often start right in about having a relationship, dating, where he's going to take her out on a date, and so forth. To the woman, this is a complete anti-mystery. The man doesn't even have her information yet and he's already telling her everything he is going to do, where he is going to take her, and what he likes to do with women. This does nothing to build any anticipation. He is laying himself in her hands like an open book, saying: *Here is everything there is to know about me.* It takes away all the mystery and challenge from her. Women want to be in a love story. Love stories are mysterious and full of building sexual tension and then releasing it at key moments. When you tell a woman everything that is going to happen, it's like telling a friend the ending to a movie they have not seen yet.

When a guy starts talking about relationships, dating, marriage, and other things of this sort, it makes a woman feel as though he is being needy, and is smothering her. They want to move away from that scene as fast as possible. Before you can start getting into declarations of love, you need to make a woman feel comfortable. She has to feel safe. You need to make her feel that she can be totally in her feminine and relax, without having to keep her guard up against your next move. The best way to do this is with laughter.

When you first meet a woman, your goal is to make her laugh and feel comfortable. You need to talk to her. Better yet, you need to engage her in talking to you. Ask her questions. Get to know who she is. Keep the conversation light and positive. Joke, banter, and tease her in a playful, non-offensive manner. Treat her how you would treat a bratty little sister who, even though you give her a hard time, she knows that deep down you really love her, but are just having a little fun. Just have a good time.

The whole purpose behind this is to get past that instant, visual interest of attraction. You are trying to engage her and, at the same time, gauge her attraction level for you. The goal is to find out if this woman is really someone you even want to go out with. If you joke around with her, or you tease her and she's nasty to you – who cares? You are probably never going to see this woman again anyway, so what does it matter? If she doesn't respond to your jokes, or doesn't think you are funny, you don't want to spend your time with her. You should always come from the place and assume that all women want you. Now of course that's not always going to be the case. Most women are not going to be single, available or into you anyway. However, if you presuppose that you're already in, it's easy to walk away when they reject you, feeling like it's their loss.

By banter and joke, I mean that you always need to be prepared to respond with a light-hearted, non-serious answer. If she says: *Do you have a girlfriend?* You might respond with: *"I always have room for one more. Are you asking me out? Wow, you're really forward."* etc., keeping a smile on your face. If she says: *Well, I think you're a jerk.* Don't argue with her. You simply need to come back with something less serious, and an "I don't care" attitude, such as: *Why, thank you for noticing!* You need to shrug it off.

Remember that you are a strong, centered guy. Something like this should not push you off your center. When you are in your place of confidence, she will often read it as funny, but cocky. Google "Corey Wayne How To Be Cocky & Charming To Get laid" and "Dominant Behavior... Gets You Laid." She wants to see if you really are what you are putting out there. She is going to test you to see if she can push you off that center of confidence. She is looking for your reaction, to FEEL your strength. If you just blow it off, you are confirming to her that you really are as confident as you portray. You have passed her test.

The other day I was at the counter of a sushi place and a girl from another restaurant in the mall came in for a pick-up order, wearing her uniform that said where she was from. I jokingly commented: *What? Are you a traitor?* After all, she was wearing the uniform of another restaurant, and here she was at the restaurant I was at, picking up sushi. I said: *Is there something I should know about the food where you work?* I could have as easily said: *Oh, so that's the secret ingredient in your desserts.* After her surprise over my comment, I was able to get a smile out of her. At that time, I wasn't looking to get her number or anything. I was just out to make her smile.

You should be friendly to EVERYONE, everywhere you go. Treat all women the same. Why? Because repetition… is the mother of skill. "Excellence is not a singular act but a habit. You are what you do repeatedly." ~ Aristotle. You never know when you are going to turn around and meet the next great love of your life. If you are this way everywhere you go, chatting up Misses Right when she shows up in your life will be just like breathing. Google "Corey Wayne Improving Your Social Skills" and "Corey Wayne The Process Of Improving Your Social Skills" and "Practicing Your Social Skills" and "Be Friendly To Everyone." You won't have to think about it. If you only wait for the ones you really like, you'll choke and walk away pissed off at yourself for not being ready and blowing a good opportunity simply because you were not prepared. "Success depends upon previous preparation, & without such preparation there is sure to be failure." ~ Confucius.

One suggestion I would like to make is go to the mall and banter with women you don't have any interest in at all. Joke and tease with them to develop your skills. What happens is when you start talking, teasing, joking and being humorous with a lot of different women, is that you get in the habit of doing it. When you come across a woman you are *really* interested in, you can just be natural.

I do it all the time. Every time I see a woman and an opportunity to tease her, I take it. It hones my skills and keeps me in practice. When I run into to somebody that I want to approach, I can act the same way with the one I am interested in, as I did with the one that I was not. Practice makes perfect.

It is a great way for you to go and become comfortable with your confidence and who you are. Talk to women in the gift shops, and the hallmark stores, or wherever you come across them. Pick the ones that you are not interested in and joke, banter, and tease them. Build your skills. Make these skills a part of who you are, while at that same time bringing a smile to somebody's face.

Ask people their opinion on gifts to buy for loved ones, opinions on dating and relationships, suggestions for cologne to wear, etc. Women LOVE to give their opinions on pretty much everything. Once you do this with the clerks and see how easy it is and how open they are to giving you advice on all kinds of topics, talking to random women or people in general at the mall will be much easier.

Go at your own pace. Start out by walking around the mall and making eye contact and smiling at people who look you in the eye and smile. Women who are single, friendly, available and who like you will look you in the eye and smile. That is their invitation to approach. Women who are married or in a relationship, who have a bad attitude, who are unavailable, etc., will simply ignore you and act like you are invisible. They will not look at you even though you know they can tell you are making eye contact. That makes it really easy. Only approach women who are friendly, smile at you and make mutual eye contact.

Once you get bored with that, you can simply take the next step and say something like, *"Hi! How are you? How's your day going? What are you ladies up to? Etc."* By asking questions and for their opinions on anything and everything, they will do most of the talking and you can simply say, *"I gotta run, but it was nice chatting with you! Have a great day!"* as you walk away and end the conversation. Once that is easy and boring for you, then simply close with, *"Hey, I gotta run, but I would like to talk to you some more. What's your phone number?"* as you look down at your phone expecting to get it. If you're really bold, you should do what I do, *"I gotta run, but I'd love to meet up with you for a drink sometime. When are you free to get together?"* and then wait for her to tell you and make a definite date. Google "Corey Wayne How To Make A Definite Date With A Woman So She Does Not Break It" and "How To Properly Set Dates." I make dates on the spot. Why? The more steps you put in between meeting a woman and making a date, the higher the likelihood that you'll never get one.

Sometimes I will be out and a woman I'm interested in will look over. I will sometimes stick my tongue out at her. It usually catches her off guard. She may stick her tongue back out at me. This tells me she is willing to be playful, and that she is interested. Other times, I might motion with my finger for her to come over. She will often motion back for me to come to her. I won't do it. I will simply shake my head and motion her back to me. I am letting her know that she has to come to me. If she doesn't, I will just shrug and ignore her. Nine times out of ten, before five minutes have passed, she has joined me. There it is – she is interested. If I were to go to her, I would have given her some of my power. At that point, I have stepped out of my masculine and let her take charge. I have stepped out of my confidence and stopped being the leader.

Watch her reactions to your joking around. If you are telling really stupid, corny jokes and she's laughing, even though you know that they're not really funny, it tells you she is interested. It's a measure of your success at making her feel comfortable, which is exactly what you need to do.

A woman has a higher level of attraction to a man she can have fun with and that can make her feel comfortable. If you are being too serious with her from the start, worrying about dating, relationships and labels, then you may be engaging your emotions too fast for her. It is a signal for her to back away and test you.

Compliments: From the Beginning

Another thing that can have a negative effect on a woman's attraction level is compliments, especially if she is beautiful. If she is beautiful, then she has been told just that since she was five years old. She doesn't need you telling her. She knows it. She sees herself every day in the mirror. There are probably 15 people she meets every day that tell her how beautiful she is. Even if it doesn't have a negative impact, complimenting a woman you just met for the first time is not going to *raise* her attraction level in you, unless you do it properly.

Many guys who are just learning to use what I teach will often get nervous and say, *"You have really nice nails."* Then they will say, *"You have really nice hair."* Then they might compliment her on what she is wearing or some other BS compliment. What's happens is their nervousness overwhelms their ability to act natural and say what's really on their mind. What happens is that instead of communicating their interest in a masculine way, they come off as robotic, uncomfortable, inauthentic, ass-kissy, phony and basically trying to use compliments as a bribe for sex. The woman feels a weird unnatural vibe and it feels like she is being clinically diagnosed, instead of authentically being celebrated and desired by a man who is used to getting what he wants.

If you're going to compliment a woman, say what you're really thinking and feeling. These are some of the things I say to women based upon how they make me feel inside: *"You take my breath away. You're intoxicating to look at. I want you. You're sexy as hell. You have a fucking unbelievable body! I want you! Etc."* Obviously, for the average guy, it will take him some time to build up to being able to say these types of things fearlessly. Go at your own pace and comfort level.

Here's another way to look at it. You don't have to lay out the compliments to a woman when you first meet her. The instinctive radar she has is already telling her you are interested. If you walk up and start talking to her, that already shows her you are interested. A guy doesn't have to tell a woman how pretty she is, how smart she is, or lay it on thick. When a woman gets compliments from a guy she just met, she starts thinking: *He's just saying whatever he needs to say.* That makes her feel as though she can't trust you. You come off as a pleaser, which is weak in her eyes. He guard will instantly go up.

What Women Emotionally Respond To

When a guy has found a woman he is prepared to talk to, the first thought in his mind should be: *My goal here is to make her smile.* That's it. Women are emotional beings. He should be in that space of feeling confident in who he is, and that he is giving her a great opportunity by coming up to speak to her. If she doesn't like him, blows him off, or treats him harshly, it shouldn't matter. Therefore, if you make her feel good by getting her to laugh, she will associate you with feeling good. We will get to more of this in the section on taking rejection personally, but the man should view it as her loss, not his.

You need to realize that when you engage a woman in conversation to read her attraction level, you are not looking for her approval. Google "Corey Wayne Seeking Her Approval Causes Rejection." It's a level playing field. You are going up to see if she is interested in you. If she's not, move on.

This is important, gentlemen. Too many men get hung up on singling out one woman to devote his attentions to. There is no scarcity of women out there. You should be concerned with finding one that does have a high level of attraction, and stop wasting your time with one that doesn't have any interest in you at all. In my coaching practice, that is one of the biggest mistakes I see guys make – getting hung up on a woman who does not reciprocate interest.

If you are single and looking to meet the next great love of your life, then one thing you should never ever do is get hung-up on just one woman until she has earned it. When I was younger and inexperienced, all too often I would get hung up on a girl I went on one date with who later rejected me, or somebody I was hoping to be with who was either a friend, or already in a relationship and therefore unavailable. This caused me to fixate all of my attention and emotional energy on someone I had very little potential with. Months and years of my life were wasted on women I essentially had no chance with. The whole time this was going on, I was constantly meeting and interacting with many beautiful single women, but because I was hung up on a fantasy, I really wasn't even in the game.

When we get hung-up on one woman only who has not earned it through her actions, we are either acting needy due to a scarcity mindset and fear of loss, or this is the pattern of how we unconsciously sabotage our own success to avoid a relationship altogether by fixating on someone who is unavailable or uninterested. We tell ourselves all kinds of lies about why we should stay focused on our daydreams and fantasies instead of realizing we have a lot of options. As a matter of fact, from a purely numerical standpoint, there are more beautiful single women in the world than you could ever possibly ask out. What you want is out there. Not only that, what you want also wants you, but you have to be in the game to score.

Busy, successful men who are very popular with beautiful women never get fixated on just one woman when they are single. Why? Since they see themselves as a prize, and act like they are the prize, women respond accordingly. They see them as a catch and are willing to chase and seduce them to get them to choose them over all of their other choices with women. They simply do not have the time to worry or think about women with mediocre or low interest who are not responding to them.

Busy, successful men communicate abundance. They come from a place of abundance. If things don't work out with one girl, it's no big deal. There is another bus every 15 minutes.

You need to learn how to come from a place of indifference. Google "Corey Wayne Indifference Makes The Difference With Women" and "Corey Wayne The Attraction Of Indifference." When you decide to approach a woman, you are going up to find out if she *is* interested in you. If she is, you are going to want to get her contact information, or make a date right on the spot. If she's not, then you are going to want to move on and find somebody that is. Guys will sit and talk all night to one woman, trying to raise her level of attraction. They completely ignore the fact that she is just not interested.

A strong, centered, confident guy is going to walk up to a woman and read her level of attraction for him. He is going to try to make her laugh, get her contact information or make a date on the spot, and then move on to gauge the interest of other women that may also be interested. It's best not to be seen getting numbers of other women by women who he just got their number from. Women want to feel special. At least more special than the other women he is dating. By the end of the night, he may find that he has ten phone numbers. Out of those ten, there will probably be only a few that are really interested. As you follow through and find they have a low level of attraction, don't bother with those women any more.

By applying what I teach, you will see that some women like you, but most do not. When you start experiencing what I teach yourself, this gives you even more confidence to do more of what's working and what I teach. Eventually, your success will improve because you will get good and spoiled at hanging with women who dig you. You'll eventually get to the point where you can tell everything about a woman just by looking at her and how she looks at you. As your skills improve and you attract better and better quality women, the women who you date today, more than likely six months from now... you won't even give them the time of day. You deserve the best you can get!

You only want to spend your time dating women that have a high level of attraction to you. The higher the level of attraction a woman has for you, the more fun she is going to be when you go out. The lower her level of attraction, the more you are going to have to work at making her feel comfortable, making her laugh and carrying the conversation. Once a guy starts learning how to gauge a woman's attraction level, he won't have to go out on twenty dates to find one woman that is interested in him. He will know right away whether to take more time with a woman or to move on to find someone worthy of spending his time with.

Before you can even think about engaging a woman's emotions, you have to get her to trust you. Trust from a woman can be a hard thing to earn, taking a long time, or it can be effortless and you can start building her trust from the start. It's all in how you approach her. As I mentioned before, using humor and encouraging her laughter is the best way to bring down her barriers and get her to open up to you. From the very start, she won't feel as though she has to keep her guard up against attacks on her emotions.

Especially in the first stages of a relationship and dating, it is important to keep things light-hearted. Keep it funny. Joke around. Keep your conversations positive and steer it away from negativity. Hang out, have fun and hook up! Keep it simple.

Guys meet a woman and they think: *Okay, I'm going to get all my baggage out on the table. Yeah, I have 3 ex-wives and I'm paying $20,000 a month in alimony. That only leaves me a $1000 a month for* *myself. It's really tough. I can't wait until my kids are 18 and I don't have to pay child support any more.*

Gentlemen, what you have just told this lady is that you are negative. You are not necessarily a fun person to be around. You are bitter and she needs to keep her guard up around you so she doesn't end up as the next focus for your negativity. You are needy and not in your center. How can a woman feel comfortable and relaxed under such an onslaught? This is the kind of crap they show in movies and TV all the time: men acting like women attracts women. Women want a guy who acts like more of a man than they do.

When a guy starts talking about his ex-girlfriend or ex-wife from the very start, a woman is looking at it from a standpoint of no emotional involvement yet. She listens and learns what it would be like for her to be your next ex. A woman is watching and gauging these things to see if it would be safe for her to lower her defenses and open up to you. You are also giving her the opinion that you are untrustworthy, since you seem to have nothing but bad things to say about the women in your past.

If you are in a relationship, making a woman feel safe and comfortable is an ongoing process. Here's a common problem many clients have when they come to me: their woman is not putting out. It's always because she no longer feels safe and comfortable in her man being the leader in the relationship.

If your wife or girlfriend is uninterested in sex or always has trouble getting wet, when before she was always initiating sex and always dripping wet any time you put your hands down her pants, this is the sign of a woman who does not feel safe and comfortable in the relationship. It means that she may be angry with you, have low interest, you may have done something to hurt her, etc.

A man is responsible for the environment and the direction of the relationship. After all, a man will penetrate his woman physically, emotionally, spiritually and mentally. If he has stopped courting her, there is financial stress, he argues with her or simply does not know how to break down her barriers when she is upset, she will shut down to him emotionally and physically. She will lose her interest in sex.

When a man does not take care of what he needs to take care of the relationship; managing money, keeping his word, understanding and communicating with her effectively, etc., she will doubt his masculine core, pull away and she will often become bitchy. Sometimes however, she may piss you off. Here's how to handle situations when women violate your boundaries: Google "Corey Wayne When She Pisses You Off."

Your job as a man is to recognize when your woman shuts down to you so you can open her back up to you through communication. Ask her what's wrong. Tell her she seems a little distant and that you want to know what's in her heart. Say things like... *tell me more, don't leave anything out, I want to understand where you are coming from, what else?, etc.* you will know when you've got to the root cause of the issue and have resolved it to her satisfaction. She will give a sigh of relief and probably say... *"I feel so much better! I'm so glad we talked!"* Until you hear those words, you need to keep digging and getting her talk about her emotions and her feelings without trying to solve the problem. For women, talking about their problems helps them resolve and work through them. Getting them to talk will also reveal if it is something you have done to hurt them. I go into a lot of detail on this subject later in my book, but I wanted to mention this here as it relates to women feeling safe and comfortable.

With a woman, you should let her do 70% - 80% of the talking. You want to ask questions and opinions. Women want to know a man is sincerely interested in who they are. They want to see that you want to know what they are all about. This is sales skills 101. People love to talk about themselves. The quickest way to get someone to like you is to ask them questions about themselves or their opinions and be a good listener. I highly recommend Dale Carnegie's "How to Win Friends and Influence People" audio series. What Dale learned and taught over a hundred years ago still works and applies today! It's timeless wisdom you should invest in.

You should be asking her where she grew up and what she likes to do for fun. Here are some good questions to ask that create attraction on dates: Google "Corey Wayne Pickup & Date Questions That Build Attraction." Find out who she is and what is important to her. You need to keep the conversation light. Stay away from serious subjects. If she presses you to talk about serious subjects, especially in the beginning, always be humorous and fun. You want to make her laugh. You want to have a good time. Fun = positive emotions = her associating feeling good and having fun with you. Your sole purpose with a woman is to make her comfortable, make her laugh, and to get her level of attraction to go up. Then you want to quickly get her contact information, or make a date and leave, which I will explain more about in a later section.

The way you get her attraction level to go up is to be humorous, have fun, show her a good time, and keep it positive. Always maintain eye contact. Keep your focus on her. When you are on a date, don't be checking out other women, the waitress, or whoever else is around. When you do that, you make her think that you are a pig, just another horny guy that's out to get laid. So your complete attention and your focus should be on her having a good time with you.

You need to raise her comfort level, and at the same time, find out everything there is to know about her. You have to *show* her that you want to know everything about her. Listen to what she says. You *will* be tested. She wants to know that you are listening to her. This is an important point with women, whether you first meet her, you are on a date, or you are in a long-term relationship. Women tend to remember every detail, while these same details tend to escape men.

It's important to listen to what she is telling you. She wants to know that these things are important to you. You'd better at least remember the gist of the conversation or there's going to be hell to pay. By listening to what she says, you are not only raising her attraction level, but you are also raising her level of trust in you.

Women Fall in Love a Lot Slower than Men

Getting back to what I said earlier, when a guy meets a woman, he can instantly have a really high level of attraction to her. Women take a lot longer to fall in love. A woman needs to trust a guy before she will open herself up to even the possibility of committing her emotions. A man is basically ready to make love at the drop of a hat, and his emotions are instantly engaged. For a woman, romance is the whole experience of the dating. It's about the mysterious love story unfolding just like in a book. Google "Corey Wayne Women Want To Be In A Love Story" and "Corey Wayne What Women Are Attracted

To In Men." She never knows what's going to happen next. It's a scientific fact that women are more attracted to men whose feelings are unclear.

It's the experience of the courtship that turns a woman on emotionally. Part of that experience is the anticipation, wondering where she stands, what's going to happen next, or when you are going to call. Some women will say they don't like these things, but I have found continuously that these things *do* have a positive effect on their level of attraction. If they are starting to wonder about you, it is also engaging their emotional input. Most women can't involve themselves in an intimate relationship until their emotions are engaged, which is the exact opposite of men.

Because it is an important point to stress, I am going to say it again: *Women fall in love slower than men fall in love.* The whole experience for her involves how you ask her out, when you call her on the phone, as well as the anticipation of what is going to happen on a date. It is where you go on a date, how you handle yourself, how you handle the others around you, and how you handle her.

Consciously or unconsciously, men and women both keep score when they meet someone, are dating someone, or are with someone they are interested in. It's not an actual scoring system, but they do keep track of the things the other person does to either raise or lower their level of attraction. Let me give you an idea of how men and women differ in their thoughts on a sample date. Women have their own rating system that is totally separate from guys' systems. Men think: *Okay. I bought her flowers – that's worth a point. I took her out to a nice dinner – there's another point. I took her dancing afterward*

– *that has to be worth another point.* See how this all adds up so quickly in a guy's mind? Bribes for sex.

The same date from a woman's point of view is going to go something more like this: *He took me out on a date. He was attentive to me – that's worth a point. He didn't check out that beautiful waitress, even when she was sort of flirty with him – there's a BIG point. He referred back to something earlier in the conversation. That means he was actually listening to what I said – I'd give him 2 points for that one. I felt so relaxed and comfortable with him. He even made me laugh – That's another 2 points in my book. I actually feel as though I could trust him more, now that I'm getting to know him. He is definitely doing the right things to raise my attraction level.*

If you want to win a woman's trust, gentleman, and ultimately her heart, you have to understand how she thinks. You have to understand what is important to her. A woman needs to feel safe to open her heart. She needs to trust you. She needs to know that her heart will be protected. The way you do that is to allow her to feel safe to be in her feminine energy, by making sure that she can feel certain you are in your masculine energy by being the leader and leading things to a successful conclusion in the bedroom.

I like to meet out for a drink first. Why? If you decide you don't like her, it's easy to leave. If things go well, then you can order appetizers and maybe dinner. Have two or three places close by that you can go to if things go well. Maybe go to a second place for darts, to shoot pool, a wine bar, bowling, miniature golf, etc. If she has a high level of comfort and you're sure you really like her, you can pick her up at her place like a gentleman. You open the car door. You take her to some place fun. The higher her attraction and comfort, the more likely you'll be able to simply go pick her up like a gentleman. The lower her interest, the less she knows you, the more standoffish she will be and the harder it will be to get to her front porch.

The key is to take her someplace fun and maybe a place she's never been before. With smartphones and a Google Maps App installed, you should always be able to quickly find cool places to go or things to see. If you take a woman to 2-3 different places in one evening, it's like the experience of multiple dates on one night. Why? Most guys go to dinner and then take her home. The average woman will sleep with a guy after 2-3 dates. Give them a fun experience at multiple places close to one another in the same evening, and you will dramatically increase your chances of scoring quickly.

Guys tend to dwell on all the physical attributes of the date, while women focus on the emotional attributes. It's the experience of having a nice dinner, drinks, doing something fun, great conversation, and just having a good time. Whatever it is that you are doing, it is the whole experience of the date, not just what you do or where you take her.

It can't be: *I took her to dinner and great, now I'm ready to go home and have sex.* Women don't operate that way. They have to warm up to you. You have to build a trust level with her, a level of comfort. Their hearts open a lot slower, because it is all about the whole emotional experience. The more comfortable they feel and the higher their attraction, the sooner they will start touching your arm, sit or stand too close where their body is touching yours, play with their hair, etc.

When a woman bumps into you or starts touching you, it means touching is okay. If you look at her lips and then into her eyes, then down at her lips and then back into her eyes over the course of 4-5 seconds when you are close, and she looks at your lips too… that means she's ready to be kissed. Kissing and making out lead to heavy petting and affection. Then you can say, *"Hey, let's get out of here and go back to my place. I've got a great bottle of wine we can enjoy (or coffee, champagne, tea, espresso, etc. depending on your drink of choice)."* Google "Corey Wayne Successfully Deflowering Your Virgin Girlfriend." If she's ready she will say yes. If not she will suggest hanging where you are. Don't get upset or you will blow it. Just keep having fun and touching, etc. Ask her again in an hour or so when the affection and making out gets heavy again.

When a guy meets a woman, often he starts coming on real heavy. He starts talking about relationships. He starts talking about dating. When a woman says to you: *I'm not looking for a relationship.* She's really saying: *Whoa… slow down. I just want to have fun. I need to trust you and feel comfortable with you before that option is even on the table.*

Again, that's why you don't need to say things like: *Oh, you are so beautiful. I had an incredible time the other night.* Coming from a guy she barely knows, one that has not taken the time to get to know her, these things mean little or nothing. Plus, they can come off as a bribe for sex instead of an authentic compliment from the heart. They do not work to raise her level of attraction. All it does is to make you look like a guy who is needy, someone that is very insecure. Plus, these are things women usually say. Be more of a man than her.

It will actually *lower* her level of attraction, and you either won't get a date at all, or you won't get a second date. If you have been in a relationship for a while, compliments without the other actions behind them can even cause her to eventually dump you, because she sees no truth behind the words. She no longer feels emotionally safe, and she will start looking for someone that *can* make her feel that way.

Women Are Like Cats, Men Are Like Dogs

No matter what you do with a dog, he is man's best friend. A dog will never leave you, no matter what happens. Dogs will come right up and demand attention from anyone, even a friendly-looking stranger that appeals to them. They don't understand the concept of rejection if a stranger pushes them away. They will come right back for more. Dogs will feel an instant attraction, an instant affection for a total stranger, and run around obeying commands at the drop of a hat.

When was the last time you saw a cat take commands from anyone?

Women are like cats. They come and go as they please... and... YOU MUST LET THEM!!! If you don't, you will destroy their level of safety and comfort with you. They do what they want, when they want, and with whom they want. You can call a cat, but it will only come to you if it feels like it. Many times they will give you that bored, sleepy stare that says: *Who do you think you're kidding?* Cats look around a crowded room of strangers and will go only to the one they feel comfortable being with, the one they know for certain will give them the affection they want. Google "Corey Wayne Women Are Like Cats, Men... Dogs."

If a cat doesn't know you, it will often run and hide. At the very least, it will stay back and watch you carefully before it decides you are worthy of its approach and attention. Cats might kind of stroll by and look over and see you, and then pretend to ignore you and move on. Then the cat may come back a minute or two later, come into the room and walk around and look at you, and then turn around and leave.

The cat may come back again a few minutes later and walk a little circle around you, maybe brush up against your leg and then take off. A few minutes later the cat may come back and go around in between your legs, rubbing up against you with its tail in the air, and then all of the sudden sit down and start purring. Cats are a lot more particular about who they will give their affection to. For some strange reason, they will even decide that the only person in the room that doesn't like cats is the only one deserving of their attention. Don't take it personally. When a woman leaves a conversation or your group, let her go. If you go after her, she will feel your weakness instead of your strength. When you don't chase, she will come back, as long as her attraction is high. When a woman senses weakness in a man, they will become flakey and unsure. When they leave and you don't chase, they will later feel attraction and come back.

In order to entice a cat to your side, you have to be patient and let *it* come to *you*. If your moves are too sudden, too quick, or too aggressive, you will send the cat fleeing from your side and into hiding. Cats have to be encouraged. They let you know when it's okay to touch them by rubbing up against you, or coming over to sit in your lap. If you don't hold the cat properly, or pet it in the wrong way, it will leave. Once that happens, it becomes twice as hard to coax it back to you.

Until the cat is coming to you and letting you know it is okay to engage it, you have to stand fast and hold your ground. No matter what the cat does, or how it tests you, you need to be indifferent. You need to let it not meeting your expectations roll off of you as though it does not bother you, or that you could care less one way or another what it does.

The cat is testing you, much like a woman tests you. If you are aggressive (a sign of neediness), then you are chasing after the cat, and it is going to run away. If you come off as weak and needy, then you are no longer worthy of their time.

Women are very much like cats. You have to get to the point where no matter what a woman does, it doesn't move you off center. You cannot move quickly or be too aggressive. You also have to treat the beautiful woman just like you would treat the woman you have absolutely no interest in. It is not about being rude to her, but you have to not let her beauty affect you. Like the cat, she is drawn to the one that seems to be least affected by her. Women, and men for that matter, are naturally attracted to the most dominant members of the opposite sex.

The old saying goes: *Curiosity killed the cat.* Cats are curious creatures. They will keep checking something out as long as they are curious about it. Once they have figured out just what that something is, they become bored and walk away. The same thing is true with women. You need to keep them wondering. You need to keep them curious. If you tell them everything about you and they can see all there is to know, the mystery is gone and they move on.

Knocking Out the Competition

One of the great things I've learned is that if you can get a grasp on being a 3% man, you literally have no competition. Once you understand these principles, you can talk to other guys, watch how your friends are with other women, and fully comprehend for yourself that only 3 out of 100 guys understand women. For a guy that is single and looking, it becomes the big realization that: *I don't have much competition at all.*

It is amazing to know that a woman went out and met 10 to 12 other guys over the weekend, and 99% of them called her the next day. You have waited a couple days to call her if making a date on the spot was too bold for you at this time. You are the one that stands out to her as being completely different. You are the one that is going to get the date with her. These other guys will never get to her front door or meet her out for a drink.

That knowledge, in and of itself, is very freeing. I love talking with women. I am fascinated by women. I find them to be extremely interesting. It is especially fascinating when you listen to them talk about guys. When they talk about the things guys do, all the needy things they do, I just shake my head. Then I have to stop and realize: *How can I be judgmental? I used to be just like that, years ago.*

For me, it only serves to reaffirm all these principles, and that alone gives you a higher confidence level. Now when I talk to women, I get the whole truth. I get beyond the standard wine me, dine me, and buy me flowers. I get beyond the partial truths because I know how to ask the right questions, and feel comfortable and confident in asking them. Women are not going to say: *I want a guy that is confident, and sure of himself.* Women want you to already know these things. If you don't already know them, they are not going to want to teach them to you. They are going to move on, and continue to sort through and qualify guys until they find one that does know it. They are going to keep looking until they find one of those 3% men. The odds are literally in your favor if you apply what I teach!

I walk through the mall now and see women checking me out all the time. Years ago, the only time that would happen was when I was with a girlfriend. It's because of their radar, because of the vibe of confidence and dominance that I'm putting out there. It's the centeredness. They think: *Wow. What is this guy all about? What does he have? What's going on over there? I want to find out about that.* They are drawn to it. If you are not in that centered place, they don't even pay any attention to you.

Do you know why it is they are drawn to that, whereas somebody else might not have been noticed? Why women notice that confidence more than anything else? Women that are in their feminine, or that want to be in their feminine, are attracted to guys that are in their masculine. It is what every woman wants. They don't want to teach you to be a man. They want to feel confident that you already know how to be the kind of man that will make them feel safe. They are looking for the 3% man.

They emotionally respond to a guy that is strong, centered, and confident, to a guy they can't have their way with. The wining, dining, and romance thing is not what they are looking for at the start. Well, it's not the complete answer. It's only part of the answer.

You have to show a woman that you are a mystery. You have to be a strong man who does what he wants and marches to the beat of his own drum. You have to be indifferent to all of the testing she puts you through. She may act as though she is turned off by something, but nine times out of ten, she is testing to make sure that you are this presence that they feel. They use playful intimidation to see if you cave or change your opinion to match hers. If she walks away, who cares? The chances are high that she will come back. If not, move on.

Women in part *do* want the guy that will do the wining and dining and romance thing once they have hit that emotional level. They don't need it so much *before* their emotions are engaged, as much as they do *after* their emotions are engaged. *After* their emotions are engaged, the romance is that masculine part of you giving them the presence that you have opened them up to receive. **Before** their emotions are engaged, they want to make sure that you are in your masculine. They need to trust it is safe to open up that emotional side of themselves and give you their heart. They are only going to do that once you have passed their tests. Plus, women are usually physically weaker than men. All women have a natural instinctive fear of being alone with a man who won't stop when they ask him to. If you demonstrate through your ACTIONS that you are a man who understands how attraction works, you'll back off when she offers resistance, but take another run at her a little while later. You should not look at her slowing things down as rejection. You should simply look at it as a temporary delay to the inevitable successful seduction.

Part IV: It's Not All About You

Making Your Ideal Woman's List of Qualities

Now gentlemen, this book is all about winning the heart of the woman of your dreams. Since we are talking about the woman of *your* dreams, in that sense, it *is* all about you. However, before you can even begin to think about being in a loving, healthy relationship, you have to understand what *makes* that kind of relationship. In this section, I am going to teach you that while it's *not* all about you that is *exactly* where you need to start.

The first thing you need to do before you even meet a woman, is you have to become clear on one major question: *What am I looking for in a relationship in the first place?* You have to understand what it is that you want in a relationship before you can get into a relationship. Let's say you want to get a new car. You go out and you buy a brand new Ford Explorer. Everyone has had this experience, where you go out and buy a new Ford Explorer, and now you're driving home from the dealership and you notice that those cars are everywhere.

The reason is that you get what you focus on in life. The reason is that when you were driving a different car, let's say a Sedan, you weren't thinking about Ford Explorers. Now that you have gone and purchased a new Ford Explorer, you're excited and happy about it. You want to go show all your friends and family your new car. Now that you are actually driving it, you are thinking: *These things are everywhere.* It's not that they weren't there before. It's that now you are focused on that particular car – that is what you are going to see.

The same principle applies to meeting the right type of person. To get where you want to go in life, with relationships or anything, you have to know what your desired outcome is. You have to know what it is that you want. This is the first thing you have to get clear. Are you looking for a steady girlfriend? Are you looking for someone you can eventually spend your life with and marry? Do you want to play the field for a while? Do you want to be like Hugh Heffner? Do you want to have three, four, five, six girlfriends? There is nothing wrong with that. That's something you can have, if that's what you really want.

Once you get clear about what kind of relationship that you want, the next thing I suggest is to make a list of what you want in your ideal woman. Take a sheet of paper and divide it into two columns – the left side and the right side. The left column is going to be all the qualities you want in a woman. The right hand column is going to be all the qualities you don't want in a woman. Imagine that technology has grown to the point where you can simply log onto the Internet, put all your criteria in, and you can simply Fed-ex yourself the perfect lady. Imagine you can have her any way you want her to be. What are all the qualities you would want in a woman? What is her eye color? What is her hair like? Is it straight? Is it long? Is it curly? Is it wavy?

What color skin does she have? Is she fair skinned? Is she dark skinned? Does she have an accent? Physically, what does she look like? Does she take care of herself? Is she real thin? Does she weigh 350 pounds? What is it that you want physically in a woman? What are her qualities? Does she have a good sense of humor? Does she have a good attitude? Is she flexible? Is she a giver? Is she easy-going? Is she fun to be around? Is she successful? Is she older than you? Is she younger than you? Is she the same age? Does she have kids? Does she not have kids? Is she a smoker or a non-smoker? Does she do drugs or not do drugs? Does she drink or not drink? Is she a vegetarian or a meat eater?

Write down your whole list. If you could have it any way you wanted to in a perfect world, what would you want in the perfect, ideal woman? Google "Corey Wayne How To Attract The Perfect Woman." In the next column is going to be all the qualities you absolutely don't want. My personal experience is that I don't want someone who is devious. I don't want somebody who is needy. I don't want somebody who is insecure. I don't want somebody who doesn't take care of themselves. I don't want somebody that eats unhealthy and doesn't exercise. My ideal woman is someone that has a good attitude, someone who's fun to be around, and someone that's a good communicator.

Make an entire list of those things that you ideally want, and then those things that you just cannot live with. Now obviously, if you write down on paper *everything* that you can think of, you might have 20 to 30 things or more in each category. From there what you need to do is go through the things in those categories and pick your top ten from each list. What you should have is the top ten qualities that you absolutely must have, and the top ten there is absolutely no way you could live with.

Next, you are going to number these items in order of importance to you. To find someone that is *all* of these things you have just listed is a little unrealistic, if not impossible. By choosing the top ten of each, it becomes more realistic. These are the qualities that are the most important to you, and the ones that you should put your primary focus on. If she has any of the other things on the list along with the top ten, consider those a bonus. By numbering these top ten in order of importance, it also shows you the highest qualities you are looking for or not looking for in a woman.

After you write this list of all these ideal qualities, write a love letter to this person you have not met yet. Close your eyes and imagine you are head over heels in love with this person. In this letter, you are going to tell her everything about her that you adore. Write it as though you were writing to this someone that is head over heels in love with you as well.

This letter should detail everything about all the wonderful qualities she has and why you love these qualities about her. This letter is another important part of attracting that person in your life. It helps deepen your focus on those things you are looking for in your ideal woman. I remember showing my list to the one girlfriend I had who was from London. She said: *My, God, I am **everything** that's on your list.* She showed me hers, and I was everything on her list. ***That*** is the power of being clear about what you want.

Becoming the Person You Want to Attract

Now comes the time to be honest with yourself. You need to think about who you are for a minute: *I'm the type of person that is very combative, and I'm not a good communicator. I don't like to talk. I don't like to work things out verbally. I like to yell and shout. I'm looking to attract somebody into my life that is a great communicator, someone that is easy-going and doesn't get upset...* Face it, gentlemen, you have to *be* the type of person you want to attract. If you do not have those traits that you want, you have to ***become*** those certain traits, because like attracts like. It is a Universal principle.

You may be able to meet someone who has the qualities that you ideally want, but if you don't exhibit those qualities yourself, you are going to turn that person off quickly. She is going to lose interest and leave. Don't lose hope on this, though. If you have a quality that you want but you haven't yet developed it yourself, **and** you are willing to recognize where your flaws and faults lie, and are open to learn and grow, then it is still possible to attract someone with that quality into your life and keep her.

However, if you are combative, for example, and have the attitude: *I am the way I am. Screw it. I'm not changing for anybody,* and you do manage to start dating someone that is a great communicator, she may try to make it work with you for a while. But over time, if you refuse to change, grow, and become a better communicator, it will only become frustrating to the new lady in your life. Eventually she is going to get tired of it and she's going to leave.

It is the same with all the qualities you want to attract. If you are not willing to work to become that quality, and to bring that quality into your life for yourself, then you need to take it off of your list. If not, you will eventually turn that other person off.

Okay, now you have made your list. Next you want to take that list and put it somewhere where you are going to review it every day. Maybe you can put it on the door to your medicine cabinet, on the mirror in your bathroom, in your day planner, on your smartphone, on your computer screen, or you can put a small copy of it in your wallet. You need to be continuously thinking about your list. By reviewing it every day, it is just like any goal that you set in life – you are going to get what you focus on. It continually refocuses you on what it is you are looking for, and ensures that you are moving in that direction.

It is like the analogy with the Ford Explorer. If you are focusing on it, suddenly you are going to start seeing what you are focused on all around you. Every time I have done this, it amazes me. I created a new list recently. I broke up with the girlfriend from London because we were just not aligned in our careers and neither one of us was willing to compromise on that part of our lives. We still absolutely love each other and have a wonderful friendship where we provide support to each other. The most important thing to both of us is that we love each other for who the other is, even though we are no longer intimate partners. This is something I will elaborate on in a later section regarding the loving way to end a relationship.

I want to stress a point I have mentioned before, because I feel it is important. Once you start working to find the perfect woman, do not expect that the first woman you meet is the one you will be with for the rest of your life. Your tastes may change. Your goals and values may evolve and change. You may find there are certain qualities that are missing on your list, or that others have become more important to you. You may find that qualities that *were* important do not seem to matter as much any more. Every relationship you go into should always be taken as an opportunity for growth and change. Eventually you will refine your list and find the exact woman that you need and want in your life.

My ex-girlfriend had blond hair and brown eyes. When I wrote down my new list, I put down that I wanted a woman who has dark hair, dark eyes, between 5'0 to 5'9, very feminine, sexy, graceful, outgoing, funny, intelligent, strong, confident, sure of herself, has a great body, in great shape, and with a great personality. I want someone that can pitch and catch with me. I want someone who, when I banter with her, is not going to collapse because she has a low self-esteem, or become insulted by every other thing I say. I want a woman that will stay in *her* center and not get pushed off, someone who gives as good as she gets.

As I finished my list, every time I went out somewhere my eyes were automatically drawn to women that fit my description. Whether I was in the mall, or shopping in the grocery store, I tuned right into what I was looking for. My awareness of what I wanted developed into a highly skilled radar that honed in on exactly what I wanted to find in a woman.

Again, it's like the Ford Explorer analogy. You will find yourself looking at women that resemble what it is you are focusing on. That's why it is so important to get clear about what it is you want. You are going to meet women all the time. If you are using a shotgun approach and you don't really know what you are looking for and haven't taken the time to write it down, it is going to be hard for you to attract the right person in your life. That's because you are not clear about what you want. That's what this exercise is all about. Every time I have done this exercise, I have met someone within 60 days. It has *always* worked for me, good or bad.

Putting the list down on paper is like goal setting. Every time you chase something in life, you should write it down so you know what it is you are going after. When you know what you are going after and are very specific about it, then that person, that resource, or whatever it is that you are looking for will eventually show up in your life. This is because of the simple fact that you are actually focused on it.

Now it is time for you to go about your daily life, whether it's going to work, to the store, out with friends, or attending some event.

While you are out, keep this thought in the back of your mind: *The type of person I want to meet – where am I going to find her?*

Where Do You Go To Meet Women?

Most men, when they are looking to meet a woman, will go to a bar, or to a night club. It is simple logic. Women go to these places for the same reason – where else could be better? The answer is: Anywhere! The bar or the night club scene, in my experience, is one of the least effective ways to meet women. This is because the women you come across are often drunk, and sometimes when you later call them, they don't remember who you were. Plus, if you've had a couple drinks yourself, it can have disastrous consequences. These are also not the type of woman that *I* am looking for.

I don't drink and party like a rock star anymore. I am no longer into that scene. But if you are looking for a woman that is because it is part of your own lifestyle preference, just be aware of the potential pitfalls of drinking and approaching women. It can definitely have its drawbacks.

I had one of those experiences about 18 years ago when I lived in Fort Lauderdale. I was up in central Florida with some close friends of mine. I was out at a bar and met a woman. We had both been drinking and we seemed to be really into each other. My thoughts were: *Wow, she's really beautiful.* It was really dark. We met, talked for a while and hung out. We were making out in the bar – and we had just met. Neither of us really knew anything about each other.

We exchanged phone numbers, and she called me a couple days after the weekend was over. We made plans and she drove down the following weekend. I remember opening the door, and it was kind of like Kramer from Seinfeld with that look of pure shock on my face as I actually thought to myself: *I had way too much to drink. It must have been really dark in this place.* This girl had driven all that way down to spend two days with me. Now I have to spend two days with someone that I am just not interested in.

Obviously, meeting girls in night clubs is not the best place. To top it all off, they usually have their guard up. Most women when they go out, especially when they go out with their girlfriends, are not out to meet a guy. They are going out simply to have fun, dance, drink, and to just get a little crazy.

The best way I have found to meet women is at weddings, art shows, seminars, private parties, social events, malls, grocery stores, trade shows or even at work. If you meet a woman in a more open, public place, whether it's in a grocery store or somewhere else, she is going to have her guard up vs. meeting through mutual friends at a party, weddings, social events, etc.

The more public a place, the more her guard will be up and the harder it will be to get her contact information, make dates on the spot and actually go out with her. Women in those situations are just not going to make it easy to meet you. Your game needs to be tight to successfully pull off meeting women in public with no mutual friends or acquaintances present to give you social proof.

I give the example of an art gallery. That can also be a very public place, but at least you know you have similar interests that can be used to approach a woman. Go places you love and do things you love. It makes it easy to talk about the environment you're both in because you both share a mutual passion and interest in it. In a grocery store, or a mall, you have no concept of anything about this woman. It makes it harder to find a common ground in order to break the ice and find out anything about her. Once you learn more from practicing these techniques, you will find it easier to approach women in these situations. This comes with practice, confidence, and when you stand strong in the fact that you own your masculinity and nothing can knock you off center.

Meeting Women on the Internet

The Internet is another way to meet available women. What I do with Internet dating is create a profile that starts out by asking the reader a question that causes her to say to herself, "OMG! He just described me!" so she will contact me first. I don't waste my time sending emails to women. When I get responses, I will respond to their email or "wink" by sending my phone number and tell them to give me a call so we can chat and maybe meet up for a drink.

She'll either call me, disappear or send me her phone number asking me to call her. I will only talk for about ten minutes to create rapport and to see if I like her enough to want to meet her. Then I simply ask her when she is free to meet up for a drink and set a definite date. If you Google "Corey Wayne The Ultimate Online Dating Profile," you can find an article I wrote with detailed instructions on my website explaining the process along with an example profile template you can follow.

You may find that women will post glamour pictures that were taken professionally 10-15 years ago. They no longer look anything like the picture you saw. Or worse, there are women out there who will post a picture of a super model as their own. They might tell you that they are really thin, they exercise, they are healthy, or this and that. In their mind they are thinking: *Oh, when he meets me, he'll love me for who I am on the inside.*

What do you do if you ever go to meet someone from the Internet for a coffee or quick drink, and they are **nothing** like their picture, and they have totally misrepresented themselves? In my eyes, that is a person with no integrity. I would say: *I don't like dishonesty, and I don't want to spend my time with people that are dishonest.* Then I would just turn around and leave. I wouldn't give that person the time of day.

Dealing with Insecurity

Now obviously, in the case of the Internet dating, this woman was dealing with so many insecurities about who she was, that she wasn't true to herself, nor was she being true to a prospective romantic interest. Many men have this same problem. They are so insecure about who they think they are that they find themselves in less than ideal relationships. Worse, they continue in these relationships because they don't have the guts to leave. Google "Corey Wayne Ways To Build Your Confidence."

With everything you will be learning in the pages of this book, you need to take the information to heart. You need to know it, to feel it, and to allow yourself to shift from a place of insecurity to a place of confidence, knowing that you deserve to have the relationship that you want in life. It is your birthright. Don't just take the information and read about being one of those 3 out of 100 men that understand women. ***Become*** one of the 3%.

I have a friend that has chosen not to take my advice, but except for what I might consider to be this small lapse in judgment, he is a very sharp guy. He sold his last company for $100 million. He has been married twice now. His soon-to-be ex-wife lives in California with his two-year-old son, and he has been dating a woman that is still married. She's been married for almost five years, and she's in her second marriage. While her husband is traveling, my friend is going to Texas and basically screwing this guy's wife behind his back.

This gives her the best of both worlds. She is getting variety with this new guy, my friend. He took her to China for two weeks with a charity he's involved in. On the way back she told him she didn't want to see him any more, and that she is going to work on her relationship with her husband.

She still sees him on her terms. My friend is getting emotionally raked over the coals. I told him: *You need to put your foot down. Tell her what it is that you want, and that if you can't be with her, then you need to find somebody new.* The advice falls on deaf ears. He is hoping things are going to change with her. What keeps him from putting his foot down is the fear that if he stands his ground, he will lose her.

The truth is, if he keeps doing what he is doing, which is being weak and going along with her agenda, he is teaching her that her behavior is okay. Eventually she is going to get rid of him anyway, because he is off his center and not strong enough. The relationship she is in with her husband was not a happy relationship anyway, even before they met. She hasn't left her husband for him, because he is too weak at this point. If he were stronger, things might have a different ending. The bottom line is that if a woman is willing to cheat on her husband and to lie, then she will do the same thing to you.

When I ask my friend: *Don't you realize this?* His response is a simple: *Yes.* The problem is his attraction level is such that he is head over heels in love with her, and she's flip-flopping back and forth between him and her husband. They are both weak, and she has no clear choice. By going along with what she is doing, he is giving away all of his power. He's not acting like a leader. I guarantee you she will be spending Christmas with her husband and not with him. My friend will end up sitting at home alone and feeling sorry for himself. Because of their insecurities, some guys will put themselves through anything.

The simple truth is that my friend is not being in his masculine. He is too caught up in need. He is at the point where he needs her. He is not loving her, and he's certainly not loving himself, either. He may feel as though he is filling all of the human needs he has, but the truth is, he doesn't feel he is good enough for her. Because of his insecurities, he is allowing himself to be abused. He is a powerful and successful guy in business. What he needs to do is learn to carry that confidence over into his personal life, and put himself back into his masculine. He needs to own who he is as a man.

Control Freaks and Abusive Men

The height of insecurity is demonstrated in the control freak, who can also be an abusive man. Women will fall for the control freak, because they initially mistake the intent of the man's control in the relationship. When he sets out from the start with: *We're going to do this, we're going to do that, I'm going to pick you up at such and such a time*, women will often mistake it as strength. Over time, once the woman is already emotionally committed to the relationship, the abusiveness tends to come out. People can hide who they really are for the first 90 days of a relationship.

When a guy is abusive and controlling, it is because deep inside, he is feeling needy and insecure. The only way he can fulfill his need for certainty in life, or in his relationships, is if he controls every single detail. His stance is to just say: *Hey, I'm in charge,* or: *I make the decisions here.* That's someone who is a control freak. Over time, that relationship can turn into a **very** abusive one, as his fear of losing control grows when she tries to express herself.

A woman initially becomes submissive when she is with a control freak, because she sees that he is strong. Over time, she realizes that he doesn't allow her to do anything. She will start to pull away and test, as women do, and he will react negatively because he is coming from a place of fear. He fears losing the person he loves, but the very fact that he fears it makes him become abusive in the way he operates in an effort to exert further control. With hope, she eventually **will** leave him.

Some guys get jealous when they are out and they see another guy looking at their woman. They get all macho and want to go beat the guy up. That is needy, jealous, insecure, and controlling. It tells a woman: *He does not have enough confidence in his own masculinity to feel he deserves to have a woman like me.* When a guy is jealous, possessive, and a control freak, usually the thing that he fears the most is exactly what is going to happen – he is going to lose her.

The Need for Certainty

One of our core human needs is our need for certainty. It can be the little devil on your shoulder that tells you to over-pursue her and blow up her phone, or that you should call her every few days to make certain she is still interested. In our desire to have that certainty about how someone else feels about us, we create the feeling that we are insufficient as a person. We are looking to fulfill our need for certainty with her approval and end up creating the appearance of neediness. What we fear in life causes us to create the very circumstances we are trying to avoid. This causes men to over-pursue and chase women away. They basically communicate through their actions, tone of voice and physiology that they do not feel like they deserve her. Eventually she has no choice but to agree.

If you are uncertain of yourself, how can you expect to keep the ideal woman of your dreams? Uncertainty is a feminine quality anyway. It is important to be aware of our need for certainty and how it can get us in trouble. Too many times I see strong, confident guys that are phenomenal negotiators in business come completely unglued when they meet a beautiful woman. It never ceases to amaze me. They make this metamorphosis from a strong, centered guy into a "man-servant, therapist or gay male girlfriend," someone who is willing to wait on the woman hand and foot. It's approval seeking behavior.

Because of movies, music and television shows, men have come to believe that they are supposed to wait on a woman hand and foot and act like a stalker to make women fall for them. They learn, basically, that if they become her do-boy, she will fall in love with them. That may look romantic in the movies, but when you try that in real life, that is not the way it happens. It actually turns them off.

Approval seeking behavior is not masculine. It is creepy stalker-like behavior.

I had a friend that worked with a successful TV anchorwoman. We were all at a baseball game in one of the VIP suites. You could tell he was very into this woman. He would ask her if she wanted something to drink, and then go back and get her a napkin. He would hover around her, attending to her every need, and then sit off to the side as though he were waiting for his next orders.

When she mentioned being cold, he offered to get her a sweater, and then proceeded to go around to every person in the box to find her a sweater, announcing that she was cold. Now my friend was a smart businessman, in his late forties, and a really nice guy. In business he was sharp, brilliant, and a great negotiator. However, when he came around this woman, he went through this huge metamorphosis, and turned into a super pleaser.

She went along with it, and took total advantage of his waiting on her hand and foot, like he was her personal assistant. He was completely different when it came to business. He lost his center around women, and it was obvious from her reaction that she would never give him the time of day if it came to his asking her out. He felt that if he did enough things for her, it would evolve into a romantic relationship. Nothing could be further from the truth. If you are a super pleaser, any woman that has a sense of strength of her own is never going to respect you as anything other than a friend.

You have to be confident in yourself and show it to a woman. Confidence says to her: *I **know** I'm good enough for you.* It gives them the feeling that you will be able to keep her safe, and she could trust herself to open up to you emotionally. She has to know you are strong, and she will test that with you, more so in the beginning than any other time. Women are physically designed to receive a man, a leader.

I like to make eye contact with a woman, and then keep it until she looks away. I will not be the first to look away. Only the most confident women won't look away. Those are the ones I'm personally interested in. When she finally looks away, I know that I have passed that first test of strength/dominance. If I were to be the one to look away first, I would be showing a submissive weakness that she may or may not test again, depending on her level of attraction to me in the first place. The more you show strength and confidence, the more you are able to quickly pass through her tests of your strength, the faster you can get her to open up to you. She needs to know you are strong and will not buckle under her testing.

When you go out on a date, you are there to be a gentleman a charming James Bond – not her approval-seeking servant. If you want to meet a woman and get into a relationship, you have to act as though you are already in one. You have to have that kind of confidence level, because that's what draws women to you. It is called *fake it until you make it*. Once you make it part of who you are, you will display that level of confidence whether you are in a relationship or not. Better yet, you will continually have a sense of centeredness that attracts women to you, without even having to try.

Staying On Track

An important concept you need to keep in mind as you are going through your daily life is about being centered. What this means is that you need to be the same way you are at work and in your business, when you meet a beautiful woman. You should treat all women the same. Be consistent with all women. You can't just turn into some weak bowl of jello. That's what most guys do. They meet a woman that they are really interested in and they go from these strong, centered guys to weak, needy, and insecure super pleasers. Most men think that being a pleaser, or being a manservant and waiting on a woman hand and foot, is a way to get her to fall for you.

The only difference in how the many concepts I am teaching may apply to you is whether you are already in a relationship, or if you are just meeting a woman for the first time. If you are already in a relationship, you will not be using the approach techniques, but the underlying principles are still the same. From the beginning, a woman is continually testing you to see if you are worthy of her time. She is seeing if you are strong enough to go the distance. If you pass her tests, she will open up to you emotionally.

You always want to be reading her level of attraction. It is important to keep building a sense of anticipation. By understanding her attraction level and where it's at, you can tell if you need to adjust what you are doing to draw her back to you. You always want to keep her attracted, and you have to avoid complacency. Google "Corey Wayne The Art Of Pulling Back To Create Attraction."

It is important to remember that the way you treat her when you are dating her and the way you treated her to get her to fall in love with you in the first place, is the same way that you need to treat her even after being married for twenty years. Courtship is on-going and it is never going to end. Always build anticipation. Avoid falling into routines. Don't go out every Friday night and take your wife to dinner. Try going out one week on a Wednesday night to do something different. Skip a week and take her out twice the following week. Always keep her wondering. Add spontaneity. Leave her curious as to when the next surprise is going to come. Never tell women what you're going to do. Let them discover it in real time.

You need to remain certain. You need to remain in your masculine, and allow your woman to be in her feminine. You have to remain centered at all times and never let her push you off that center. By maintaining this certainty within yourself, you are also maintaining a long and lasting relationship with a woman you truly want to be with. You have earned the right to the relationship you truly deserve.

The Purpose of All Relationships

When you can find certainty within yourself, you are not only giving yourself the gift of a wonderful and loving relationship, but you are also giving the woman of your dreams the strength she needs to trust. You are giving her the gift of allowing her to open herself to being in her feminine. Better yet, she is able to be in that place of her feminine especially for you.

No matter what the relationship, the foremost thing that needs to be in your mind is that you enter into a relationship to give. You give because that is who you are and you expect nothing in return. However, you need to always watch what you do get in return, and decide if it is acceptable to you. Give your gifts from love. Love never requires anything in return. It is in the giving that makes you feel good. True love does not have attachments. You give freely, without caring what comes back in return. You give of yourself because that is who you are.

When you want to get into a relationship, you have to go into the relationship not with what you can get out of it, but with what you can put into it. The purpose of all relationships – and this is not only for your intimate relationships, but also for your friendships, the people that you work with, your kids, or any other relationship you have – is to go into those relationships to give. If you go into a relationship focused on what you are going to get out of it, you will be placing expectations on some new person that you just met. Ninety nine percent of the time, they are not going to live up to your expectations and you will end up disappointed. This causes us to suffer because we want reality to be other than it is.

Many guys go out with a woman and think: *Oh, I took her to dinner, and showed her this great time. She had fun. I am expecting to have sex at the end of the night.* Instead of looking at what you are going to get out of a relationship, you should be thinking: *How can I give to this person? How can I contribute to her? How can I make her life really amazing by having fun with her?* When I go out with a woman, my primary goal is for her to have a good time. My contribution is to make her laugh, make her feel comfortable, and make her happy – that's it. The feeling she feels while she is with you is what she is going to associate with you.

Everything else takes care of itself. If both people are focused on what they can give to a relationship, the relationship is going to flourish. But if one or both people are focused on what they are getting out of it, it's not a relationship. It's a transaction. You might as well go get a hooker, if that is what you are looking for. If you are going out on a date with an expectation of having sex, go get a hooker. It is a lot cheaper, and there are no emotional attachments. If you truly want to have somebody you can share your life with, someone you can love, someone where you can enrich their life, and have fun with – *that* is the purpose of a relationship.

If you select somebody that has the same kinds of qualities as you have, she is going to focus on making you happy as well. When both people are focused on simply giving to the other person and not worrying about what comes in return, the needs of both are going to be fulfilled, regardless. It is in the giving that needs are fulfilled.

I said this before, but it bears repeating: *Once a guy really understands women and is able to get into a relationship, he is going to realize that every relationship is an opportunity for growth.* You can understand and become the type of man you are totally capable of becoming. At the same time, you inspire and help her grow into everything she is capable of becoming as a woman.

Making Lasting Change

Lasting change should be a goal. I know some of you are asking: *Why should I change all these things?* Think about this for a moment: *What is the outcome? What do you want out of a relationship? Why do you want this?* Now take a sheet of paper and split into two categories.

One of my favorite speakers, Tony Robbins, says: *People will do more to avoid pain than they will to gain pleasure.* For the purpose of this exercise, take one column and write down: *Okay, if I don't change all the things I have been doing in the past, here are all the consequences.* List all the painful things that will happen: Well, if I won't go up and ask a woman with confidence what her phone number is or set a date, I will never get the kind of woman that I want in life. I will never have the type of relationship I really want. 20 years from now I will still be wondering: *What is it like to have the type of woman that I really feel I deserve?* Or maybe: *If I don't change my behavior, my wife has already told me that she is going to leave me.*

You know, it is ironic that most guys will never seem to have time to spend with their wives, but they always have time to go visit the divorce lawyer. They make the time for those types of things, but they don't make the time for things that really count while they still have a chance to avoid the pain. What *are* all the painful consequences of not changing your behavior? Write them all down. If you do not change what you are doing, what are all the negative, painful things that are going to happen?

For the other category, consider: *What are all the pleasurable things that can happen if you change your behavior?* This is for all the good things that can happen in your life. Along with your list for your perfect woman, you need to review this every day.

So what do you do if you just met someone last night and you just *know* she's into you? Normally, you want to call her right away. You feel as though: *Oh, God, if I don't call her right now, I am going to burst. If I don't call her, she is going to get pissed off and mad at me.* The bottom line is that you have to ask yourself a simple question: *Have you ever gotten the type of woman you really want and have been able to keep her, based upon what you were doing in the past?* Of course, the answer is going to be: *No.*

I went through all these same dilemmas when I first started following these concepts. Honestly? I felt as though I wanted to pull my fingernails out, as opposed to just waiting a few days to call her, or to resist the urge to ask her where I stood constantly. It absolutely drove me nuts. The truth is that it gives *her* that sense of anticipation, which is what she wants. What I later learned was that the women that I had met and liked and who also had a really high level of attraction to me were going through the same thing. They kept thinking: *Why hasn't he called? I thought he really liked me. I don't understand. Maybe I know someone who knows him... Maybe I should call him.* It's a scientific fact that women are more attracted to men whose feelings are unclear. Besides, if you are a busy, successful guy you should have lots of options with women and an active life.

Who knows? If she has **really** high attraction for you, she may call or text you before those several days have passed. So it is important to follow these concepts. I will say this with confidence: It is really freeing when you go out on a date to know: *Wow, all I have to do is ask the questions, and keep my answers to the questions that she asks me positive, light-hearted, be funny, be humorous, get her to laugh, and just have a good time. If you're not good with banter and humor, or you're just starting out, stay away from the sexual innuendo. Why? There's a really good chance you will say something stupid and create an awkward moment.* You want to banter back and forth and always respond to her tests with playful humor. I discuss this in detail on the many articles and YouTube videos on my website. It's better to hear how I say things in my videos because it just does not translate well to write about it.

Now you are starting to get an idea of what you should be doing. In the next sections, I will start to show you how these are applied in practical situations. If you are already in a relationship, you have to start dating her again and treat her like you did when you were courting her. She will fall back in love with you and everything will fall back into place. All of these things work. They will make an incredible impact on not only you, but also your dating and relationship life. After all, it's **not** all about you. But it **is** where you have to start.

Part V: Making Your Move

Approaching the Beautiful Woman

One of the things I pointed out earlier is that when a guy meets a woman, he instantly knows whether or not he has a high level of attraction for her. With a guy, he's ready to throw his arms around a woman at the drop of a hat. With women, it is the experience of the courtship that turns her on emotionally, and all the anticipation leading up to the actual dating part of the relationship.

It starts when you first meet her, with how you present yourself and how you are dressed. Do you take care of yourself? Do you look good? Do you wear nice clothes? Do you dress nicely? Are you clean-shaven, or do you wear a beard with confidence because it's who you are? Do you have nice cologne on? Do you take care of your appearance and your body? It's not the clothes but how you wear them that make the man.

When you are out and see someone you are interested in, you need to first start looking for signs of attraction. If you look at her and you think: *Wow, what a very beautiful woman. I'd like to meet her.* Look at her body language. Look her in the eyes. Is she looking back? Is she checking you out? What does her body language say? Is she facing you? Does she smile when you look at her? Or if you look at her and she catches you looking, make eye contact and smile at her. Does she smile back? Does she look away? If she smiles at you that *may* be an invitation that says: *Hey, I find you attractive. You should not hesitate to walk over and say hello. Google "Corey Wayne The Best Pickup Lines Ever" for some good openers to use. You should also Google*

"Corey Wayne Rejected? The Best Comebacks Ever" for great comebacks when a woman is playful, tests or challenges you so you can playfully recover when things go sideways.

What you need to do at that point is walk over to her. Before you even **say** anything to her, keep watching for signs of attraction. Is she facing you? Is she looking you in the eye? Is she not paying attention to you? The more attention she gives you the higher her level of attraction to you is. It is really too soon to rate at this point because you haven't even talked to her yet. Her attraction level can't really be determined until you do, but you can pay attention to the more subtle signals first.

By understanding all these little things, you will eventually become aware of where you stand even before you start talking to her. The place where I am at in my life is that now, when I look at a woman, I know right away if she is interested. I also know right away if she is single. The more you work with these techniques and make them a part of you, the more highly developed your instincts become. Remember, she already knows how to do this with you. This only levels the playing field.

Women use their radar all the time. Most guys are completely clueless. They think a woman is interested mostly because they are projecting their own level of attraction onto her. They think that by talking to her, buying her drinks at a bar, etc., it will make her all of the sudden become interested in them. A woman who is out for the night will let a guy buy her drinks all night long, even if she's not interested.

A man also makes the mistake of talking to a woman he has just met about all the bad relationships he has had in the past, thinking maybe she will feel sorry for him. He will tell her that he is single and completely available, because he thinks it is what she wants to hear. He believes these are the things that are going to turn a woman on.

Nine times out of ten, the things he is saying are actually turning her off. Nature has already taken care of attraction; it's not a choice. Most guys simply talk women right out of liking them. He is sounding needy, and is not coming from a place of strength. He is laying himself out like an open book and is building no anticipation for her to find out more about him later. There is no mystery, no inner masculine strength, and no chance in hell that she will go out with him.

So as you are walking over and approaching this woman, you are watching. Is she looking at you when you are approaching? If she's not, it doesn't mean anything, but again, the more she's staring at you, the more she's checking you out, the greater the chance is that she has a high level of attraction for you, and is single and available.

Now let's say that you are completely noticing her and she looks at you. If her eyes then go to the left or the right and she just continues doing what she is doing, that usually means that she's not finding you appealing enough. If you are walking toward her, and she looks you in the eye, looks down, back up at you, and then away, that usually means that she has an attraction to you.

Here's a great technique to create rapport and create the vibe where women will feel comfortable coming up to you when you are out at a bar, or a night club: You and whoever you are with should take your drinks and make a couple laps around the bar. Whenever you see a group of women, especially ones you are interested in, you can walk up to them and say: *Hey ladies, how are you doing?*

At that point, hold your glass up and toast, or touch glasses together. Then ask: *Are you ladies having a good time?* When they reply: *Yes*, you are going to say: *Great!* Have that level of confidence and courtesy that says, without actually saying it, that you may have something to do with the club, or you may be the owner, owner's son, or something along those lines.

From there, you are going to leave and move on to the next group of ladies and do the same thing. Make a couple trips around the bar. When you come back through to the same group, just toast them again and keep on moving. Now you have shown up, toasted them and asked if they are having a good time, and then walked away. You leave them wondering: *Who are those guys? They look like they're having a good time.*

After that, seat yourself at one of the tables in plain view of everybody. Simply hang out with your buddies and let the women come to you. Now you have gone around the bar and have created a connection with all these groups of women. Every time you walk back by these groups of women, you have made yourself more familiar to them. Just by "clinking" your glasses together in a toast, you have increased their awareness of you.

Eventually some of these women are going to start coming up to you. They are going to want to hang out and talk. You have created a setting where they are comfortable. You haven't gone up and started hitting on them like every other guy in the bar is doing. You are just a guy that is out having a good time. You and your buddies are now seen as guys that are completely different than every other guy in the place. You are out to have a good time, and are not there to chase the girls around. You have made yourself approachable.

When you are going around, they may stop you and talk to you. Or maybe when you are going to the bathroom, they might stop you and try to talk. You have just created an opportunity to get to know them, get their information, and leave. You are taking two steps forward, one step back. You are not hanging around like every other guy is doing. You are coming in slowly, and then you are gone again. You are building anticipation, being indifferent and being mysterious.

I also have a detailed article on how to get women to approach you first on my website. You don't have to do any approaching with that technique. It's great to use if you are just starting out, you're too shy to approach women or if you're just lazy and want women to come up to you first. Google "Corey Wayne How To Get Women To Approach You First." Make sure you watch the video on "Body Language That Attracts Women" on the website also. It's essential to get the body language and vibe right so women will come up to you first.

The Path to Success

So as you walk over to a woman, the most important thing to consider is what you are going to say. Most guys will walk up and say: *Hi, my name is Corey. What's your name?* That is a blown opportunity to see whether she is interested in you or not. When you walk up to a woman that you have not met, you need to walk up and simply say: *Hi. What's your name?* Wait for her response. She may say something along the lines of: *My name's Jessica.* At this point, you are not going to volunteer and say: *Well, my name's Corey.* When she says: *My name's Jessica,* you are only going to say: *Well, Jessica, it's nice to meet you*, **without** volunteering your name. This is the first test of you reading her level of interest.

Now compare the following two responses. 1) *Oh, it's nice to meet you.* 2) *It's nice to meet you. What's your name?* Which one do you think shows more interest in you – the one that wants to know your name? Or the one that just says: *Nice to meet you?* Nine times out of ten, the one that wants to know your name means she has a higher level of attraction. In other words, she finds you attractive or appealing. She wants to know who you are. That is a good one I learned from Doc Love (doclove.com).

Your whole goal when you meet a woman is to judge her level of attraction for you. If it appears that she has a high level of attraction, then you want to get her phone number, a way to get in contact with her. You are **not** going to tell her that you are going to call and ask her out on a date. Just the very fact that you are asking for her phone number tells her that you are interested. She knows what that question means.

A woman knows instinctively: *The reason he's asking is because he likes me. He wants to take me out.* It is not necessary to volunteer and say: *I'm going to call you. I want to take you out on a date.* Your interest is already obvious to her just by the fact that you have walked over to her and asked her for her name. The fact that you want to take her out on a date is obvious at the moment you ask for her phone number. It is common sense to the intuition of a woman. It is only guys that do not see it as common sense. This is what I am helping you to develop.

What I do is either set a date on the spot or start your first date right now. You can say, "When are you free to meet up for a drink?" Make definite plans and get her number before you leave.

After you have gone up to her and introduced yourself, you are going to talk, joke, and banter with her. An important thing to keep in mind – and guys in sales understand this – is the person that's asking the questions is the one in control of the conversation. Your goal is to find out as much as you can about her and give her as little information about yourself as possible. Respond to her questions with light, joking answers and ask her another question. Google "Corey Wayne Pickup & Date Questions That Build Attraction" for good questions you can ask and topics you can discuss. The idea is not to interrogate her with questions like a robot, but to ask questions that elicit interesting and fun answers that can lead the conversation into fun and unexpected directions. You are leaving yourself as a mystery in her eyes. You are building her anticipation to find out who you are and anything about you.

You want her to dig for information. The reason you are not going to volunteer straightforward answers is that you want to see what her level of attraction is. If she has interest, she is going to ask you questions: *What do you do? Where do you work? Where are you from?* The more personal the questions are that she asks, and the more enthusiastic and inquisitive she is about you, the higher her attraction level.

Do not ask her if she has a boyfriend. She may have a guy she is dating that she recently broke up with, or maybe she is considering breaking it off with him.

A woman that has very low interest in her current boyfriend may just be waiting until she meets someone new to break up with him. There are many women that will not break up with a boyfriend until they have a replacement. This is one of those things that stuns guys who have been married for ten years and their wife just left them: *How can she be dating another guy the week after we split up?* It is because she stayed with you until she was over it, and then waited to leave until she had somebody else lined up. So, you don't need to ask her if she has a boyfriend. It is unimportant. Her questions, her body language, how she acts toward you – this is going to give away what her level of attraction is.

Your goal is to make her laugh and make her feel comfortable. Only talk about positive things. You are not there to talk about how you just got dumped by your last girlfriend or how you never seem to get the type of girls you really want. Trying to make her feel sorry for you is **not** going to make her want you more. It will have the opposite effect and turn her off to you. Keep it funny. Keep it uplifting and positive. Don't talk about serious subjects. Don't talk about marriage, politics, or religion. Make her laugh. Joke, banter, and tease her. Just have a good time with her.

Here is the next key to success: *You don't need to spend more than five to fifteen minutes with her.* After five to fifteen minutes of talking with her, joking around, and having fun, if you are successful at making her laugh, then she is showing a high level of attraction. Think about it. If you are telling really stupid, corny jokes and she is laughing at them even though you know they are not that funny, it tells you she really likes you.

The next step is to get her phone number. Ask her something along the lines of: *Jessica, I've got to run, what's your phone number?* After that, just stop. Do not say anything else. You are going to listen and pay attention to her response. If she just pulls out a piece of paper, or a napkin, writes down her number and gives it to you, that shows a high level of attraction. But you also need to pay attention to how she is engaged in that process. You need to watch her body language and how she gives you her information.

If she gives you her e-mail address, her work number, her cell phone number and she tells you the best times to call her, that is definitely a sign she's interested. The more a woman likes you, the more she is going to help you. If she really likes you, if she's really interested in you, she is going to make it very easy for you to meet up. If she is giving you all her contact information, she wants to make sure if you do call or want to get in contact with her, that you *are able* to get in contact with her. She may even ask you for your number as well.

The more information she passes along to you will give away what her level of attraction is. If you ask her for her number and she says or does anything other than giving you the number, the lower her level of attraction is and the more she's going to resist you. The less she likes you, the more difficult she is going to make it for you to get that information. She may like you enough to go out with you, but she may test you to see if you're strong enough for her, especially if she senses any weakness in you.

If she has a low level of attraction, say she sees you as a 5, on a scale from 1-10, she might come back with something like: *Why do you want my number?* Or: *You're very forward.* It is also possible that she may ask you for your business card. If a woman won't give you her number and instead asks for your business card, it shows she's not too interested. Most women will put that card away and never look at it again, or just simply throw it away.

We will take a look at how these attraction levels work, and how to judge her attraction level later in this section, but this is a very important point that I need to make: *If a woman only perceives you as a 4 or below on a scale of 1-10, there is nothing that you are going to be able to do that will convince her to go out with you.* At that point, you are wasting your time.

If her attraction level is a 5 and above, she will ask you personal questions. She will be making eye contact with you. When you are talking with her, how is her body facing? Is she turned toward you or is she turned away in the escape position, as though: *I hope one of my girlfriends comes up and pulls me away from this guy, because I don't want to talk to him any more.* Is she standing extra close? Is she bumping into you when you are talking? Is she touching your arm when you talk? Is she playing with her hair? Is she exposing her neck to you? These are all signs that show her attraction level is a 5 or higher. If you ask her for her phone number, she doesn't hesitate at all and gives you her number, that is a good indication that her attraction level is a 5 or higher.

An attraction level that is below a 5 is basically the opposite of all those things I just mentioned. She doesn't ask you personal questions. She doesn't ask you what your name is when you say: *It's nice to meet you, Jessica.* She kind of keeps her distance when she's talking to you. She is looking away, as though distracted or disinterested. She gives you one word, or short answers.

For example, when you say: *Where did you grow up?* Response: *South Florida.* Question: *Oh really? What was South Florida like?* Response: *It was nice.* That shows a low attraction level as compared to: *Oh, I loved growing up in South Florida. I went to high school down there. It was just so blah, blah, blah...* If she likes you, she will talk to you. Again, the more she likes you, the easier she makes it.

A woman is rarely going to come right out and say: *Hey, you're a really good looking guy and I want to go out with you. I want you to ask me out. Here is my number and all my contact information. I am available Sunday through Thursday, and you can call me. I'll go out any time you want, and I'd like to do anything you want that's fun.* This is just not typical. Women like the mystery. They like the process of dating. They want to discover, and they want to be discovered. They want and expect you to be a man who is a leader. Women don't want any responsibility for sex, setting dates, picking where to go, etc. That is why it is up to you to lead things to a successful conclusion in the bedroom. Invite them on a date; don't tell, sell or ask them if they'd like to go out with you. Assume all women want you and act accordingly; even though all women aren't going to want you, it's a much stronger position to assume they want you rather than to sheepishly hope that they want you. It's a subtle difference that makes a big difference in how you ask.

This also means they don't want to know everything about you when first meeting you. Most guys, when they meet a woman, spend a lot of time telling her everything about them. In essence talking her right out of liking them by talking too much. At that point, you have totally taken the mystery out of it. Now that she knows your whole life story, what does she need to go out with you for? If you go out on a date, she already knows everything about you. There is nothing left for her to discover. You have taken it all away and made it too easy for her. You are predictable and boring.

A woman doesn't want it to be easy. She wants to be able to pull that information out of you. She loves to fish. She loves to work through the whole process with the thought: *What am I going to find out next about this guy? Where's he going to take me?* Make no mistake, it is a process with a woman. You need to put her in that space of anticipation. Why do you think women read all those romance novels about mysterious strong men? Duh!

If a woman asks you: *Do you have a girlfriend?* Again, that is a sign of high attraction. How do you respond to a question like that? Do you have a girlfriend? You are **not** going to say: *Well, I broke up with my girlfriend two years ago and I haven't had a date since.* The best response is not to say: *No, I don't have a girlfriend.* When she asks: *Do you have a girlfriend?* Just say: *I'm just dating and having a lot of fun right now... or... I've always got room for one more... or... Can we get to know each other a little better before we start talking about relationships?* That can mean that you have five girlfriends. That can mean you have one. It leaves her wondering and helps to build the anticipation of what she may find out about you.

Just remember the key point that I mentioned earlier: *The one who is asking the questions is the one that's in charge of the conversation.* The goal when you first meet a woman is to read her level of attraction and to get her phone number so you can later call to take her out; or if you've got really big balls, make a date on the spot. You are not going to tell her you are going call and take her out. You are not going to give her any hints about what you may or may not do on a first date. You are simply going to ask for her number. When you are entering her number into your phone, text her yours also. Why? She may text you first if you wait a few days to call. Another good way to do it is to give your phone to her so she can put her number in as you're asking for it.

Once you have achieved that goal, you are going to say: *Well, I've really enjoyed meeting you and have a great evening, Jessica.* Give her a hug goodbye, and then move on. If it is a party or a social event and there are other beautiful ladies there, you are going to want to get as many numbers as possible. You don't want all these women to *see* you getting phone numbers from different women, so be discreet about it. Women like you more if you've got options, but you want her to feel like she is the most special out of all the women you're talking to; not just another notch in your bedpost which will cause her to reject you.

Because again, you may read a woman's level of attraction and think she is really interested in you, but that may not be the case. You may meet a woman that's great, you call to take her out, and then find she is in the process of breaking up with another guy, or she may be going back to her ex-boyfriend. She may have originally displayed a high attraction for you and then you try to ask her out and all of the sudden she seems totally turned off. You don't know what is going on in the background.

The key is that you don't want to get hung up and hold attachments to one particular lady until she does all the things right to warrant you devoting all of your time and all of your energy to her. Guys will meet a woman, they haven't even gone on the first date, and they already start imagining themselves married to this woman, what their kids are going to look like, all the fabulous vacations they will take as a family, what they will be doing on the first date. Guys will do all this before the night they met this woman is even over. You do not really know until you call her and you take her out what her level of attraction and her emotional availability is.

In the movies they always show: *You are going to meet this one woman and it is going to be this be-all, end-all relationship.* I have news for guys. When you start dating, or even when you first meet somebody, what you want now and what you want a year from now may change. You may decide you want something or someone totally different. Sometimes a relationship just runs its course and it's time to move on. This is because when you get to that place where you *know* you can have any woman you want who has a high attraction level in you to start with, and you *know* how to own her heart, it gives you a lot of choices. So basically, once you get her phone number or set a date, you are going to walk away from her. Unless you are going to turn your initial meeting into the first date and seduce her that night.

The Many Shades of "No"

When you first meet a woman, one of the things she might say is: *I'm not looking for a relationship.* One of the reasons a woman says this is that a lot of guys come on so heavy when they meet her. They start talking about girlfriends. They start talking about dating and all this other stuff, and she starts thinking: *This guy is needy. This guy has no confidence and is weak.* Women come up with generic responses to these situations because most guys will not take no for an answer. The women will reject them because they start to feel like they will lose their freedom if they start seeing them.

Another thing about women that you have to understand is that they are never going to say: *I don't like you. I am not attracted to you, and I wouldn't go out with you if you were the last man on earth.* Very few women are blunt enough to respond to a man's advances in this way. The reason most women will not directly tell you they are not interested in you is because men have pretty much made them that way.

When a man has met a woman and is really into her he will ask for her phone number. If she is not into him, she could say: *I'm sorry, but I'm not interested.* Too many times, the typical man's response is something along the lines of: *What do you mean you're not interested?* If she replies: *I'm just not interested.* He will often push the issue: *What do you mean? Are you saying you don't like me?* At this point she is getting uncomfortable and she tries to explain: *Well, you're just not the type of guy I would normally date.* He, in turn, starts to become indignant about it: *What does that mean? I'm not good enough for you? I'm not good looking enough for you?*

How do you ever get anybody to go out with you if you have that kind of attitude? It's pretty arrogant and weak, don't you think? Every woman has met a guy that has acted that way in her life, the guys won't take "no" for an answer. So she, indirectly, is hoping that he will get the hint and understand the "secret language" that she is speaking to him. Women are emotional beings and simply don't want to hurt your feelings or create an awkward moment. Instead, she uses a roundabout way of saying: *I'm really not interested.* Women will even sometimes give you their phone number, because they do not want to lie to you, but they also want to avoid the typical man's confrontational behavior. They know that later, through voice mail, they can just screen you out and hopefully you will get the hint and go away.

If they think you may be a real nuisance, they may even give you a wrong number. This brings another point to mind: *When a woman gives you a number, don't stand there and call it to see if it is a legitimate number.* Some guys will actually do this. It is so needy and insecure. What it says to her is: *I really don't think I am good enough to take you out, and I don't really think you are interested in me. I want to make sure right in front of you that you are not lying to me.* Right away you are telling her that you don't even trust her. Just confidently text yours to her as you're standing there so she has it and tell her you are doing it.

At that point, you are done, even if she gave you a real number to begin with. You just lowered her attraction level, and it may have been high to start with. When you eventually *do* call her, you are going to find out whether she likes you or not. After all, who cares? You don't want to waste your time and energy by going out and getting emotionally hung up on a woman that has no interest in you. Google "Corey Wayne Single? Don't Get Hung Up On One Woman." You only want to spend your time with a woman that has a high attraction level, because she will make it easy to date her, and she will be a lot more fun when you do. You will not have to work so hard.

Again – It's Not All about You

The place where you always want to come from, not only when you are in the relationship, but also before you have met someone, is to not take rejection personally. You have to go through life, give your gift, give your presence, and give who you are. People are either going to accept you or not. You can't take it personally. It's a numbers game. You have to get through the no's in order to get to the yesses.

If someone doesn't want to go out with you, or you thought someone was really interested enough and it turned out that they weren't – you can't take it personally. At the end of the day, the ones that really like you are going to help you and they are going to be with you. The ones that don't like you are not going to be with you. It is simple logic.

What if you have been dating for several months, you have been doing everything right, you keep giving, giving, giving to your woman, and she's not giving back? Tell her how it is that you want her to give back to you. What if she still doesn't do it? She may not be a giver. It just may not be her personality. At that point, you can decide: *I am not being treated as I ideally see myself being treated.* You can make the decision whether or not to leave the relationship. Most of the time women are the ones to break up with guys. Women are usually the ones to file for divorce. Guys are usually the ones that get dumped, without realizing why they got dumped in the first place.

If a woman doesn't have a high level of attraction to start with, if it is not a 5 or higher, there is nothing you can do. No amount of talking to her, joking, teasing, is going to do anything to make her want to be with you. It is important to understand that. Attraction is NOT a choice.

You may walk up to talk to a woman, and she may be rude to you. She may say something like: *I do not find you attractive. I would never go out with you.* You have to approach the situation with a response that shows you really don't care what she thinks. It doesn't matter.

You could say something like: *You are entitled to your opinions, and you know what they say about opinions.* Or: *I'm the most attractive unattractive guy you have ever met.* Or even: *I just like to make people laugh and smile. I'm sorry you are having such a bad day that you would go out of your way to try to hurt someone's feelings. Hey, I'm sorry you got up on the wrong side of the bed this morning. Have a great night...* and just walk away. Don't waste your time. Google "Corey Wayne Rejected? The Best Comebacks Ever."

No one is ever going to say or do anything that is not a direct reflection of how they feel about themselves in a given moment. If a woman is nasty to you, she could be testing you, or she could have had a bad day. Maybe she just doesn't want to be approached. Keep in mind that you are a strong, centered guy, she just threw a big barb at you, and you deflected it.

Meeting women is a numbers game. Some women are not going to like you and some women are. You have to be indifferent about it and not let it get to you.

Handling the Pressure Points

While your goal is driving you to meet the kind of woman you feel you deserve, this also means you want to be screening others out. You do not want someone that is a user or into only material things. If a woman asks: *What kind of car do you drive? Not that it matters...* It says it really does matter to her. Tell her you rode the bus, walked, came on skates, etc.

If she asks where you live, tell her something silly like: *Well, actually, I was hoping to move in with you and have you support me and wait on me hand and foot.* Be silly, outrageous, or be stupid. Do not give these types of obviously materialistic questions a straight answer. There are women that look for security and will marry a guy they do not love. These types of women are only looking for security and don't care who *you* are or what you are all about.

If a woman tells you looks are not important, point out some unlikely man in the bar and ask: *What about that guy?* A lot of women will respond with: *He's not my type,* even though she has never spoken to him before. It shows that looks are important to her. It's not that she is necessarily being dishonest with you, but it does give you further evidence of what I mentioned before: *What a woman **says** is not necessarily what she responds to.* Google "Corey Wayne Do Women Understand... Women?"

If a woman asks: *Do you have a girlfriend?* Be playful. You do not want her to think you haven't had a date in 2 years. Respond with indirect or playful answers like: *I'm just out dating and having fun.* Or: *There is always room for one more.* When you come off with confidence, she may further test with: *Are you a player?* You could reply playfully: *Sure, I play sports.* Or: *I played sports in high school.*

If she gives you the: *That's not what I mean.* Look at her with curiosity and ask her straight out: *What **do** you mean?* The point is, that no matter what her question, no matter how she tries to test you, you can't let her think she can get under your skin. Keep it positive. Keep it playful.

When a woman tells you: *Well, I don't date guys who are players.* You can ask her straight out: *Who said I wanted to date you?* Or: *When I meet someone who is worth my time, I will be exclusive with her. I haven't determined whether I want to go out with you or not.* At that point start asking her: *Why **should** I go out with someone like you? Are you hitting on me? Are you fun?*

The whole point to these questions is that she may or may not be interested. The lower her attraction level, the more she will test you. Pay attention to her reactions. Don't be offensive or angry, but show that you could care less whether she likes you or not. Have ***her*** try to prove to ***you*** why she is worth your time.

Another one of the things that women will actually test guys on is to see how firm they are in their position. The guy will say something to the effect of: *Oh, I like blue colored cars.* She might respond with: *I don't like blue colored cars. I like red colored cars.* Some guys will turn around and change their opinion to match hers, trying to please her. They think that's what she wants. He will then say something like: *Well, blue really... Now that I think about it, I actually do like red more than I like blue. I guess I have to agree with you.* They will change one of their core beliefs on things they want to match that of the woman.

She is trying to see if she can get you to change your opinion to match hers. If you go along with it, you are being weak and failing her test. What it tells her is that you will go along with anything she says. The challenge for her is now taken away, and she will move onto the next guy.

Timing is Everything

Okay, so now you have gone out and collected phone numbers. The next question is: *When do you call her?* Most guys, predictably, when they get a number on a Friday night, they will call the girl the next day. Some will even call that night. All this tells a woman is that you are needy. It displays your insecurities in big, bold, neon letters. It tells her you are not centered, you are not confident, and that you haven't even gone out on your first date with her yet and you already can't live without her.

All women have been with guys like that, and it will turn her off to the point where she is probably not going to even bother to call you back. She may talk to you if you manage to get her on the phone, but she will never go out with you. She perceives you as being needy, and for her, that is a big turn off.

Wait to call a woman for the first date if you did not set it up when you first met her. Don't call her the very next day. By doing this, you are already building anticipation, and setting yourself apart from all the guys that did call her right away. If I meet a woman on a weekend, like a Friday or Saturday night, then I might wait to call her until Tuesday or Wednesday to ask her out for the following week.

You should be busy anyway. Act as if you are busy as hell even if you are not. Act like a guy whose dance card is already pretty full.

If she does have a high level of attraction for you to start with, and you don't call her that night or the very next day like most guys predictably do, it's going to cause her attraction level to go up. Let's say she gave her number out to ten guys. If nine of them called the next day to ask her out and you didn't, she is going to wonder: *I wonder why that guy didn't call. I know I'm beautiful. I've got these nine other guys calling. What's the deal with that?* You are making her wonder about you. When she's wondering about you, it is having a positive effect on her level of attraction. Remember, it's a scientific fact that women are more attracted to men whose feelings are unclear.

You are being a mysterious. You are being different. That is what all women are dying for. They are dying for a guy that is not needy, one that is not going to be jumping all over a chance to go out with them like they're the last woman on the planet, someone that they can pitch and catch with, someone that's strong, and someone that they can't have their way with. This is kind of what the bad boys do. What is the draw of a Brad Pitt, or any actor that gets up on stage all the time? What is it that draws women to guys like that? Masculine energy is about purpose, drive, mission, succeeding, accomplishing, breaking through barriers, achieving goals, etc.

It is power. It is confidence. It is danger. It is leadership. It is mystery. It is the feeling: *I don't think I could ever get my way with the guy, and that makes me feel safe. This guy could protect me.* Women want a strong, centered guy. Google "Corey Wayne Women Want To Feel Safe & Comfortable" for a detailed article and video I did on the topic.

A good rule of thumb on when to call a woman is this: If you met her on a Friday or Saturday, call her on Tuesday or Wednesday and set up a date for the following week. By the time you actually go out, it may have been a week and a half. If you met her on a Sunday thru Thursday, call the following Monday or Tuesday and ask her "when are you free to meet up for a drink?" The goal is to leave days where she is going to be wondering about you, anticipating your call, and raising her level of attraction.

The Test of Time

There are several reasons why you wait to call her if you're not making a date on the spot, which is what I always do now. However, I know the average guy just starting out might be too terrified to risk that kind of rejection to his face. The first reason to wait to call is to build the anticipation of your phone call and leave her wondering. The second is to test her level of attraction again. These first stages of getting to know a woman and asking her out are all about testing her level of attraction for you. This will let you know where you stand, and whether or not she is even worth your continued effort.

So now that you have built her anticipation, you are going to call her. When you do call, if you get her on the phone, you are going to say: *This is Bob.* You are not going to say: *This is Bob Smith. We met the other night. I was wearing a purple shirt and it had pink polka dots on it, and we were at such and such a party. We were talking about this and that...* No. You are simply going to say: *Hey Jessica, this is Bob. How are you?* Then you are going to shut up. You want to see what her response is. Her response is going to tell you everything about her level of attraction for you.

Now if she says: *Oh, Bob. I was wondering when you were going to call. I thought maybe you lost my number or something.* Remember, no guy does this to her. First, this tells you she has really high attraction for you. Second, it tells you she has been thinking about you, and you have just caused her attraction level to go up even more.

If she says: *Who?* You are going to repeat: *This is Bob.* You are not going to tell her your last name or where you met or anything. If she says: *Where do I know you from?* You need to think about this. You have already thought about what your kids are going to look like, where you are going to take her on this first date, how you planned to get a limo, and all these amazing crazy ridiculous things. Then you call her and she doesn't even remember who you are. That shows that she has a very low level of attraction.

In this case, I have actually told the woman: *I'm sorry. I must have the wrong number.* I am only going to go out with women who are saying: *Oh, yes. I was wondering when you were going to call.* I am only going to spend my time with somebody that is really into me. If she has already forgotten you, then her attraction level wasn't high enough to begin with. At that point, you just need to move on.

Common sense says that you didn't lose her number, you have been thinking about her all week, and then you call her and she doesn't remember who you are. Do you really want to spend your time with someone like that? Even though she doesn't remember you, she still may agree to go out with you. Someone like that is going to have a real low level of attraction, and you are not going to have as good of a time as you would with someone who remembers who you are and has been eagerly awaiting your phone call. If someone doesn't remember you,

you need to move on, because you're wasting your time. It shows an attraction level that is below a 5.

If she does remember you, then you have determined that she has a higher level of attraction for you. When you met her, your goal was to get her phone number, get her number after setting up your first date or to start a date on the spot. It all depends on your skill level. Now that you have her on the phone, your goal is to get to meet up for a drink, coffee, etc. You want to actually be able to take her out on a date.

At this point, most guys think: *Oh, I've got to talk. I have to get her to really warm up to me. I have to talk to her on the phone a couple times for two to three hours, and then I'll finally ask her out.* No. Anyone in sales will tell you that the phone is for setting appointments, not for giving out information.

Let's assume she remembers who you are and she was wondering when you were going to call. Now you are going to be direct, confident, and you are going to say: *Jessica, when are you free to meet up for a drink?* You are not going to say: *I was wondering if you would like to go out sometime.* That shows your schedule is wide open, you don't have anything else going on, please pick a day where I actually get to spend time with you and have you grace me with your presence your highness.

A strong, confident guy is sure of himself, is direct, quickly gets to the point, makes decisions and knows he can have other women if he chooses. Why should this one woman warrant his time? You want to know that if you go out with her, she is going to have a high level of attraction. Once again be quiet and listen for her response.

If she says: *I'm free Wednesday or Thursday.* You are going to respond: *How about we meet at blah, blah on Thursday at 8 pm?* Provided you're both free then. When she says, *sure!* Then say, *Great, Jessica. I look forward to seeing you Thursday night at 8. If you get there first, get us a table. If I get there first I will get us a table. If something comes up I will call you. Otherwise, I will see you at blah, blah. Does that sound good?* Her: *Yes.* That's it. You have now set the date, and you have been direct and have definite plans. Google "Corey Wayne How To Make A Definite Date With A Woman" and "How To Properly Set Dates" for more examples, videos and detailed articles I have written on the subject analyzing other guys' emails.

If she has a real high level of attraction, this is pretty much how it will go. The lower her level of attraction, there are certain things you are going to hear. If you are asking a woman out for a date, she makes the plans, gives her address and then gives you the: *Call back to confirm* or she says: *What is your number in case something comes up? Please call me later in the week to confirm, etc.* That means it is more than likely that something is going to come up and she is going to cancel.

My response in this situation is something along the lines of: *Jessica, I have a really busy schedule, and I would definitely like to see you, but if you can't make definite plans with me, then how about we just do it some other time?* Then you are going to wait for her response. It is what we call in sales, the ***Take Away or Negative Sale***. If she says: *Yes. Give me a call and we'll make it for some other time…* her attraction is low. If her attraction is high, she will be more likely to say something along the lines of: *No, I just wanted your number. I definitely want to see you.*

Again, you are going to be quiet and wait for her response. I have had women do that, and then keep the date. That tells me that her level of attraction is probably a 5. At that point she is testing who you are, and by answering her test in this way, you are showing confidence. It makes her think: *Okay. He stood up to me. I'll go out with him.*

Remember, as far as you are concerned, you are a confident, good-looking guy. You want someone to be as excited about going out with you as you are with them. If someone is giving you a wishy-washy answer, she is saying that you are not a big deal to her. She is really not willing to go out of her way to spend time with you. If that's the case, then you don't want to spend your time with her.

When you ask a woman out on a date and she maybe calls you on the day of the date and tries to change the plans, she is testing you to see if you will give in to her. There was this one woman that I had gone out with before, and I had totally blown it with her. A couple years later, I ran into her, after I had figured things out about women.

Now before I go any further with this, I do not want to give you the impression that you can just go back into your little black book and pull out all the women you have ever gone out with and try this. This is for more of a specialized circumstance, for if you come across her sometime in the future. Under normal circumstances, once something has ended with someone and they blew you off, forget about it and move on.

I am including this story because it happened to be a special case. It is also a good example of how women test when they know there is a weakness. I am talking about a woman that I was really into, but at one time, her level of attraction to me was very low to start with.

I was going out to dinner with a friend one night and I saw her. We were walking down the street and she happened to turn and face me. She gave me this kind of a stunned look, because we hadn't talked in a couple years and she had pretty much blown me off. I just looked over at her and grinned, and stayed where I was. We were only about ten feet away, but I didn't go over to her.

I called over to her: *Hey, How are you doing?* She walked up and gave me a hug and we talked for a bit. I asked her what she and her friend were doing, and they told us they were going over to this one bar. The old me would have followed them to the bar, but the new me just said: *It was good seeing you. We were going to go have some dinner. You girls have a good time.*

My buddy and I turned and headed to the restaurant, which was not far away. At one point my friend turned and looked. She was just standing in the middle of the street, staring at us with a look on her face that said: *I can't believe he just walked away from me.* It was something totally out of character. She had expected me to be all over her like a cheap suit, the way I had been in the past. It totally confused her.

When my buddy told me this, I replied: *Of course. She can't believe that I just walked away from her.* I did my two steps forward, one step back. I hung out long enough to tease her and joke with her and then turned and walked away and went about my evening with my friend. I didn't ask for her phone number or anything, because my attitude was: *Maybe she'll call me or e-mail me.*

This was on a Friday or Saturday. On Monday, she e-mailed me. She told me that she had been pretty shocked to see me again after all these years. One of the things that helped was that at the time, I was sort of a small-time, local celebrity. I had an infomercial that ran regularly on television. It created a bit of mystery and intrigue that made her reconsider: *What about this Corey guy? Something is different about him.*

The biggest part was that I walked away from her, which was totally out of character from how I used to be. I didn't e-mail her back right away. She was in radio advertising at the time, and she suggested: *Maybe I can come by and talk to you about radio advertising some time.* I thought to myself: *No. We're not going to be talking about radio advertising. Now I have a chance to make up for how I screwed up a couple years ago.* She left her number in the e-mail, and I waited to call her back until the next day.

All I said at that point was: *Hey, this is Corey.* There was that little awkward silence that said it was an: *Oh my God, he called me,* kind of moment on the phone with her. We talked for a couple minutes. She was talking about advertising, and I gave her a cocky little attitude and said: *Oh, so you wanted to get a hold of me to sell me some advertising, huh?* She went on to explain how she just got into the business, and how her bosses said she should try to talk to me. So I told her: *Great. How about we go to lunch Thursday? I'll pick you up at 12.*

She responded: *You're going to come here?* I told her: *Yes. I'm going to come pick you up.* She was hesitant, but we made the plans. She was very reluctant in how she handled the whole thing, but she gave me the address. I could tell that she was testing me because I had been so weak all those years ago. She wasn't accepting of the fact that I could have changed that much, so she was testing me as much as she could.

Again she said: *You're going to come here?* I told her: *Yes. I am going to pick you up, and open the door, and I'm going to take you to lunch and we're going to have a good time.* She said: *Okay. Call me before you come just to confirm.* I told her: *I don't call and confirm dates or appointments. I'm a very busy guy. I would like to take you to lunch. If you can't make a definite commitment to get together with me for lunch, then we will just have to do it some other time.*

After that I paused and waited. She backed up and said: *Okay.* I didn't make the actual date until the next week because I really wanted to stretch it out and heighten the anticipation. The day came, and I had told her I wasn't going to call and confirm. About an hour before the time came, she called me. I picked up the phone and she said: *I just wanted to make sure you were coming.* I replied jokingly: *Of course. I said I would. Are you telling me that you normally go out with guys that would stand you up?* She laughed and I added: *If I tell you I'm going to do something, I will. I am a man of my word. You should know that by now.*

I went and picked her up, opened the car door and the whole nine yards. We went to lunch, sat down, and we never did talk about business. She did about 80% of the talking, and I was teasing her, joking with her, and bantering. Every time she asked me a question, I would give her a short answer and would joke back and forth with her.

Later, I asked for the check and ended the lunch date. When we got back to her office, I didn't get out and walk her to the door, because it wasn't a formal date. She said: *I had a nice time.* I replied: *Yes, it was fun. It was good seeing you.* She looked at me expectantly, as though she was waiting for me to ask her out again. Tip: don't do lunches. Hangout, have fun and hook up. Do evening dates. If you want to be her lover, do things a lover would do. It's hard to seduce a woman when you go to lunches, but like I said this was a pseudo sales pitch from her that I wanted to turn into a date later.

I used to do this a couple years ago: At the end of one date, I was already asking her out for the next one. You should never do this. It shows that you are weak, needy, and you are afraid if you try to call again that she won't go out with you. You should always leave her wondering where she stands with you, raising the level of attraction and anticipation.

She e-mailed me that afternoon and said: *You never did answer any of my questions.* I sent her back a joking response. She e-mailed me again a couple days later and I called her. She suggested we get together again and have some drinks. So I made the date with her and asked for her address. She asked: *You're going to come to my house?* I told her: *Yes. That's what a gentleman does. He comes to your house, picks you up, holds open the car door, and treats you like a lady. It is the way you should be treated.*

She told me: *I can't have you coming to my house.* I said: *Why not?* She replied: *Because.* I told her firmly, but jokingly: *Just give me your address.* I was treating it as though she were being a little silly. The way I asked was from the assumption of: *of course she's going to give me her address without any hint or doubt she would.* She gave me her address, but she also threw the "call back to confirm" at me again. I told her: *Hey, I would love to go out and have drinks with you, but if you can't give me a definite yes, then I'm not going to make plans with you.* She backed up and said: *Okay. What time are you coming?* I told her seven o'clock, and we made the date.

When the day of the date arrived, she sent me an e-mail and told me she was feeling funny about it. I found out she had just broken up with her boyfriend, and she was getting a little wishy-washy about going out, and then wanted to meet me wherever we were going. So I did the "take away": *If you don't feel comfortable, then why don't we just make plans some other time?*

She called me a bit later and told me she really wanted to see me. The problem was that her ex-boyfriend was starting to show up at her house unannounced, and she felt kind of weird about the whole thing. The last thing I wanted to do was to show up to take her out and have some jealous ex-boyfriend show up. So in this particular case, I went along with her changing the plans. Normally I wouldn't, because it's usually a test of your strength, but this situation warranted a change of plans.

So we went out to dinner and had a great time. Then she proceeded to tell me what effect everything I did on the last date had on her. It had definitely raised her attraction level with each thing I had done, every step of the way. We sat there talking and never did end up ordering dinner. 11 o'clock came around. I lived near downtown, so I suggested that we go back to my place and order pizza.

I took her back to my place, which had a full liquor bar, icemaker, blender, etc. up in the loft, and we just hung out. After a while, I just knew it was time from all the signals she was giving, and I told her: *You need to come over here and kiss me.* She just smiled, grabbed a napkin and wiped off her lipstick and came over to me. Needless to say, we had an incredible evening.

She tested me more than a woman would normally do with a guy because I had botched things so badly the first time around. This time,

I did everything right. We had an awesome time and got to know each other. It had everything to do with being strong and confident, and being willing to walk away if she pushed me too far. That was the feeling I gave her. Until a woman knows that and feels it, you will never own her heart.

When you do finally go out on a date with a woman, you are going to have a lot more fun with someone who has a high level of attraction as opposed to a lower one. The lower the level of attraction, the harder you are going to have to work on the date. You are going to be asking all the questions, and it is going to be harder to get responses out of her. If you go out with a woman who has a high level of attraction in you, she will be asking you tons of questions, and is going to be totally into you. Those are the type of women you want to spend your time with. They make it easy.

When you call to ask a woman out, you are going to set a definite date, and you should not be on the phone more than five minutes. The phone is for setting appointments, not getting to know someone. I will have women ask: *You're not going to call me before you come?* I usually answer in a light-hearted manner: *I am the kind of guy who keeps my word. I am making plans to see you next Tuesday, and I'm definitely going to be there. I'm looking forward to it.*

The best thing about this is you don't have to call back to confirm, so you don't have to worry over the next several days whether or not you are actually going to be able to get a hold of her or not when you call back to confirm. Nine times out of ten, if a woman gives you a call back to confirm response, you are never going to get her on the phone again. You will end up getting her voice mail. The whole time your attraction level has been creeping up higher, and she wasn't even interested in you to start with.

It is all about building anticipation and raising her attraction level to you. She doesn't know when you are going to call. You have not told her when you are going out. Then you call and you make the date. You have waited a few days. Her attraction level has gone up, and now you are making a date for sometime the next week.

Once you have made your date, it gives you such a comfortable feeling to know that you have done everything right to this point. You have played your cards, she tested you a little bit, and you passed her tests. Now you have a definite date. One of two things is going to happen. Either you are going to show up at her doorstep to pick her up or meet her out somewhere and you will go out and have a great time, or she is going to cancel the date. Or she may call and try to change the plans a little bit.

If she calls and tries to change the plans, again, it is a sign of low attraction. If you met in a very public place or on the Internet, then it is more understandable that she would want to meet you away from her home. The point is, once again, the higher her level of attraction, the easier she is going to make it for you to go out on a date with her. The lower the level of attraction, the more roadblocks she will put in your way, or the more testing she will do.

Another example of the testing I have experienced was with one woman I had been dating. Sometimes when a woman has a lower level of attraction, she might call and try to mess with the plans a little bit. This woman called me about three to four hours before I was supposed to go pick her up. I was driving in my car, saw it was her calling, and answered.

She said: *Where are we going tonight? I'm going to be out and about doing errands and other things.* I think part of it was that I hadn't talked to her since I had made the date with her a week before. Part of me realized she was worried I wasn't going to show up, since she hadn't heard from me. It was having a positive effect on her anticipation. She was trying to play it off, and said: *I wanted to know where we are going.* I told her: *That's for me to know and you to find out when I come and pick you up tonight* in a playful tone.

She responded: *Well, I kind of wanted to meet you out tonight.* I asked: *What for?* She replied: *Because I'm going to be doing errands.* I asked: *Oh yeah? What time are you going to be done with your errands?* The time she gave me was well within an hour or two before I was supposed to come pick her up. I told her: *Don't worry. You'll be ready by the time I come to get you.* I was ready with the responses. That was one of the things I was starting to get at that point: *Always be prepared.*

She kept trying to get around it and have me meet her out somewhere, and gave me the: *I'll call you when I'm on my way kind of thing.* I simply said: *How is a guy supposed to come pick you up, open a car door, and be a gentleman if he's meeting you out somewhere?* Finally I told her: *We are supposed to go out at seven o'clock. I will be there at seven o'clock, and I'll see you when I pick you up.* She said: *If you come to my house, I'm not going to be there.* I replied: *If you're not there, you're not there. I'll take your mother to dinner, then. I don't care.* She laughed at that and I said: *I'll see you at seven. Gotta go – bye!*

I hung up on her. She tried, she tested, and she didn't get away with it. I passed her test. We went out that night and had a really great date.

It's All in the Numbers

The chart you are about to view is a guide, not a definitive answer. It gives you an idea of how to interpret her answers and responses to you. It will give you a *feel* for where she is at regarding her level of attraction for you. It is important to keep in mind, if your wife or your girlfriend has what you think to be an attraction level of say, 7-8, she will also be doing things in the categories below that. In other words, if her attraction level is a 7, she will also be doing things from the category at 5-6, and 6-7. It may not necessarily be all the things in the lower categories, but you will find that she will do many of those things.

Always underrate her attraction level. It must be a 5 or better to start with or you have no chance. For the married guys and those in long term relationships, you must watch for her dropping attraction level. As it drops, she will do less of the things she did when she was in love with you. Your goal is always to keep her in the 9-10 range. Watch for touching, affection, compliments, and I love yous all to start dropping off as her attraction level drops. As it drops, she will also start testing you more and more. It is her way of saying: *Hey, step up and be the man you are totally capable of being.* She will accept nothing but your best.

It is imperative to understand where a woman's attraction level is at, because this is *the key* to developing your radar, that intuitive sense of *knowing*. At some point in the relationship, you are going to become complacent. It happens to all of us. It even still happens to me.

I remember one time a few years ago when I had a girlfriend. At that point, I was feeling pretty high and mighty about how I had come to understand women. I was on a date with her once with a bunch of associates that worked for me. We were at the table having some drinks, and she proceeded to tell me how unhappy she was. She was upset that I was not displaying affection or verbally telling her how I felt about her. She was really angry about the whole thing.

I was stunned to the point where it left me speechless. I was so sure of myself, and it made me realize that I had become completely complacent. I had not been paying attention to the fact that she wasn't as affectionate and she wasn't as loving. I instantly started thinking about how she had been treating me for the past couple weeks and realized that her attraction level had gone down all the way from 9 to somewhere around 7.

This was a big shift. It dropped slowly, but I just kept doing one thing wrong after another. My old habits were coming back. All I could think was: *Here I am, knowing all this stuff about women, and yet I am doing things that I know better than to do.* It took me a couple weeks, but I did get things turned around and back on track. This happened to me about six months after I thought I really had things figured out. I had thought things were going really smooth and then this came along and totally blind-sided me.

With my understanding of the concepts of this chart, the things she did, and where her level of attraction lay, this whole thing really gave me a wake up call. Without it, I probably would have kept going as I did in the past, until things could have been too late to salvage. It is important to always stay aware, and to always underrate her level of attraction. You need to pay close attention to where she is at with her attraction level, because it drops slowly.

You especially need to pay attention if you are in a relationship where you live with someone, or you are married. You are together every day and it becomes so easy to get caught up in your daily life. All of the sudden you wake up and realize: *Wow. I've really been messing up here. My lady is no longer in love with me, and things aren't going that well.* At that point, you have to turn it around quick and do all the things that made you successful in the first place. A good weekly communication exercise you can do with your girl to keep things going well is to Google "Corey Wayne Rate Me Baby!"

Do not take this chart as an itemized list, but rather view it from the perspective of concepts. It is not a definitive guide that says: *Hey, she just touched your arm, now she is in the 7-8 range.* You have to look at all of the things she is doing. If you determine that she is in the 7-8 attraction level, she will also be doing some of the things in the 5-6, and also the 6-7, as well as in the 7-8. Even then, if she is in the 7-8, act as if she is in the 6-7. Your goal is to get her to the point where she is completely, head-over-heels in love with you, which is in the 9 range.

You have to consciously be aware of getting her attraction level up there, which means doing all the right things. For guys that have been married, or have been in a long-term relationship, it means all those things you did in the courtship, being your own man, building anticipation, being completely unpredictable, are necessary. This is not only when you are dating, but also when you are making love to your lady, as we cover in a later section. All these things are absolutely critical to maintain her love over the long term.

It is something that you can't ever let up on. If you are going to be in a long-term relationship, you are going there to give. What you are giving is those things that make her happy and keep her in love with you. If you are not willing to do that long-term, you shouldn't be in a long-term relationship.

0-4: One of the things most guys do not understand is if a woman has no attraction to you – you have no chance of going out with her. You have no chance of her falling in love with you. If she does not like you enough to begin with, nothing will happen. She may go out with you only to use you if she is that type of person or if she has a really low self-esteem.

When you call her the first time to ask her out after waiting a few days after meeting she does not remember who you are. When you ask her for a date she won't agree to a specific day or time or she gives you the "call back to confirm" response. She won't give you a specific date. She tells you she is busy: *Let's make it for another night* instead of countering with a specific night she is available. If she cancels without bringing up rescheduling it's a sign of low attraction.

Or she says: *I'm too busy. I don't have time. I have to get my head together. I need to find myself. I don't want a relationship. I'm not sure where I'm able to be at this point in my life. I'm not into dating anyone right now.* What she's saying is: *I just don't like **you** enough to date you.* She doesn't ask you personal questions. She doesn't ask you what your name is when you say: *It's nice to meet you <whatever her name is>*.

She sort of keeps her distance when she is talking to you. She is looking away, kind of disinterested. She gives you one-word answers. Like when you say: *Where did you grow up?* Response: *South Florida. Oh really? What was South Florida like? Oh, it was nice.* She also will call and break your date at the last minute with lame, wishy-washy excuses.

When you are talking with her, how is her body facing? Is she turned toward you or is she turned away in the escape position, as though thinking: *I hope one of my girlfriends comes up and pulls me away from this guy, because I don't want to talk to him any more.* Is she making eye contact? She cuts your dates short and it seems as though her thoughts are elsewhere. She may simply walk away when you are talking to her.

5-6: She will give you a hard time about giving you her personal information. She should be making eye contact with you and look like she is interested in what you have to say. When you ask her personal questions about where she grew up, she tells you and then adds: *Oh, I loved growing up in South Florida. I went to high school down there. It was just so blah, blah, blah...* If she likes you, she is going to want to talk to you. Again, the more she likes you, the easier she makes it.

She may try to give you a call back to confirm your date, which you will not accept. You will stand your ground and answer accordingly as mentioned earlier in this section. If after standing your ground on the call back to confirm she accepts, then you may be okay. You won't know for sure until you are actually at her front door or meet up with her, since she could break the date at anytime prior to that.

She also may call at the last minute to try and get you to change the plans. In that case, unless it is an emergency, I may just cancel the date altogether and do the "take away." I would respond: *Well, it sounds like it is not a good time for us to get together so let's just do it another night.* If she backs up and keeps the plans as they were, then you just passed her test. If she says: *Okay, let's do it another time,* without naming a specific time and day, then wait a full week before calling to make another date. If she pulls the same thing, then you know her attraction level is below 5 and she is out for good.

6-7: This is usually the range where most girls that really like you will be. She will give you her contact information with little or no hesitation. She may give you several ways of contacting her: email, work phone, cell phone, times to call, etc.

7-8: She leans in close and bumps into you. She touches your arm. She is really interested in what you have to say and laughs at all your stupid jokes. If she is complimenting you: *Oh, that's a really nice shirt you're wearing.* It is not so much the shirt. It is her way of saying: *You look really good. I like the way you look.*

8-9: She is calling you and pursuing you. She is saying: *I can't wait to see you again.* She is pursuing you heavily, and calling you to say: *I miss you. I can't wait to see you. I had a great time last night.* She gives you her contact information without you even asking. She will ask for advice about problems. That comes because she trusts you, and has a high level of confidence in you.

Most of the time when a woman talks to you, she is not looking for your advice, she just wants you to listen. But when she comes out and says: *This, this, and this happened... what do you think I should do?* That is her way of asking for advice. If you are unsure you should say, *do you want my advice or do you just want me to listen?*

9-10: Love starts at 9. She will say things like: *Where is this going?* Which means: *When are we going to get married or become exclusive?* If she says: *I love you*, that puts her in the 9 range. In this range, she is very affectionate. When you pick her up she jumps in your arms. She kisses you. She wants to hold hands. She wants to have her arm around you. She is all over you. She just can't seem to get enough of you. Being with you is like a drug to her. She will do just about anything you want.

She buys you gifts, writes you cards, leaves you notes, builds you up to others, defends you, etc. (This only applies if she is a giver. Some women can be totally in love with you and if they are not a giver, they will do none of these things.) She is calling you all the time, or calling you once or twice a day to say: *I can't wait to see you again. I had such a great time.* That is telling you: *Hey, I'm wide open. I want to see you. I want your attention. I want all your presence.*

When a woman is in love she wants your attention all of the time. She thinks about you and sings about you and is totally consumed by you and thoughts of you. She tells you all the time how much she loves you. She tests you very little and when she does, they are easy tests to pass.

The following story is a prime example of just how easy it can be when a woman has a high level of attraction for you. After reading this, ask yourself: *Why **wouldn't** I want my dating life to be this effortless?* When I first met this woman, she gave me her phone numbers and actually asked me for mine. I never even had to ask for her number, she just volunteered it. From the first moment I met her, I maintained my composure. I had just started learning and understanding women and was really getting it.

We had just met and we ended up talking all night. We were out with the same group of people for the evening so it was impossible for me to get her info or make a date and just leave. She was touching my arm, getting real close, and whispering in my ear. She would stand so close that we were bumping into each other. She talked about wanting to go out. She was very aggressive. I played my cards right, letting her do all of the talking, and the anticipation built.

Two days later, when I hadn't called her, she called me. I had built the anticipation so much that her attraction level had gone even higher. She e-mailed me and I responded, keeping it real short. I named the time and the place to meet for dinner, and we met out and we went from there.

First of all, she had a really high level of attraction to start with, probably in the 7-8 range, which is pretty rare when first meeting a woman. She was calling me, pursuing me, and suggested we go out for drinks. I met her out at a restaurant, and I remember being really into her. She had beautiful red hair, greenish brown eyes, and an amazing figure. She was drop dead gorgeous, bubbly, and she liked to laugh. I was enchanted with her.

I remember driving to meet her and just knowing I had been playing all my cards right. When I showed up and met her at the restaurant, she was sitting in the lobby. I had only seen her once before, the night I had first met her, and she absolutely took my breath away. She came up and gave me a big hug.

We went and sat down. I was really excited to be there and could tell she was excited, as well. We had a couple glasses of wine, and then had dinner. She must have done at least 90% of the talking. I was fascinated with her. It had been a while since I had been out with someone I had felt that way about on the first date. We just sat at dinner while she chatted away for a couple hours. I just kept asking her questions because I was so into her. I wanted to know everything about her.

I was also building the anticipation. I wanted her to wonder what I was all about. Every time she asked me a question, I gave her a short, funny answer and then I would turn it back around and ask her another question. She would go on another five minutes about something else. She was an outgoing person, and just loved to talk. I was not leaning forward on the table. I was leaning back in my seat with my legs spread and taking up too much space to let her see how nonchalant and confident I was about being with her.

I often make it a point when I am initially dating someone, to be the first one to end the date. Again, I want to leave her wanting more. It is like the pro football player that retires at the top of his game. Here we have had this great date, and the anticipation has been building, building, building… and then I'll ask the waiter for the check, and I'll pay.

I could tell the look on her face was saying: *Oh, I'd really like to sit here and talk some more*. While it was not quite disappointment, I knew she could have sat there a lot longer and talked more. We got up and walked out. I turned to her, starting to say: *Where did you park?* I had really done a great job of building that anticipation. I think I only got a single word out before she just grabbed me and kissed me. We started making out right there, only three feet outside the front doors of the restaurant.

Inside I was going nuts and just loving it because I was totally enamored with her. I walked her over to her car and we made out some more. Then I opened the door for her, let her get in and said: *I had a nice time.* I remained totally composed, even though inside I wanted to jump up and down and do some cartwheels in the parking lot. I left feeling amazing.

I did everything right on that first date. The whole time, from the day I met her, until the time we had our first date, because she had such a high level of interest to begin with, and she was a very aggressive, beautiful, confident woman, she just couldn't help herself any more. She just had to kiss me. Of course, I didn't have any problem with that at all. The next day she called me again.

This is what happens when you play all your cards right, especially when you have a woman that has such a high level of attraction for you to start with. Why would you want to bother with someone who doesn't have that high level of attraction, when life can be this effortless? I only had to show up, hang back, and say very little. I was so relaxed and it was so easy to be with her, because she *made* it so easy. I was not feeling confident on the inside, but I showed her that on the outside.

You become comfortable with being yourself. You make it part of who you are. Sooner or later you own it. And you have to own it, because if you can't maintain it later in the relationship, if you ever let that down, then you are not the person she thought you were in the first place. She will see weakness, test, and pull away. This makes you start to pursue her, which drives her away even more. Learn how to read her attraction level and make it a natural part of who you are and what you do, and you will win the heart of the woman of your dreams with little effort.

Part VI: The First Step

Your First Date

You do not have to be extravagant on your first date. The idea is to hangout on a date, have fun while you are hanging out and hook up by making a physical move. The process of seduction is to get closer and closer to a woman until you ultimately end up inside of her. You should make dates in the evening that can lead to having sex at your place or hers. Most women sleep with men by the 2nd or 3rd date. You can to take her to dinner, meet up for drinks, coffee, miniature golf, shoot pool, an art museum, etc. You want to go somewhere that facilitates conversation, laughing and having fun together.

Going to the movies, loud music venues, lunches, etc. are not a good idea. You want the opportunity to get to know somebody. Talking creates rapport. If you go to a movie date, the only time you get to talk is in the car on the way to and from the movies, or if you're meeting her outside the theatre before the movie or after it's over. At the end of the date she doesn't know anything about you, and you don't know anything about her. When you are in a dark theater, you can't read her body language. It is important to go someplace where you are talking and interacting with each other, so you can read where her attraction level is at, and work toward raising it.

When she starts touching you and getting close, you should then go for the kiss. Kissing leads to heavy petting which leads to you saying: *hey, lets get out of here and go back to may place for a bottle of wine, etc.* A good way to know if she is ready to be kissed is to look into her eyes while she is talking or you are talking. Then gently look at her lips and then up into her eyes, then back at her lips and then back into her eyes again over the course of 4-5 seconds. If she looks at your lips at anytime when you are doing this, it means she is thinking about kissing you. Be the leader and go for it. Women won't usually make the first move.

A lot of rich guys will say: *I'm going to fly you to New York in my private plane.* Any woman would love to go out and do stuff like that. Before you spend your money doing these kinds of things, you want to make sure you are going out with someone that has a high level of attraction for you, personally. Take her to nice and fun, but inexpensive places at first, until you really get to know her and you know that she is really interested in you.

It is important, especially for guys who are successful, not to spend the night talking about your achievements, how much money you make, what kind of car you drive, what your watch is like, or how much you spend on wardrobe. Most guys talk too much and ruin attraction. None of this causes attraction. If a guy starts talking about all these accomplishments, what it says to a woman is that he is insecure about who he is as a man. It's approval-seeking behavior. Google "Corey Wayne Seeking Her Approval Causes Rejection" for a detailed article and video I did on the subject. She reads it as a deflection away from who he is as a person. He comes off as needy, insecure, and unsure of himself.

The only type of woman that will respond to this type of thing is a woman who is looking to use a guy or one that is looking for security. The most important thing to remember on your date is that a woman wants to know you are interested in her as a woman, not just her body and looks. You show her that by asking questions about her and leading the conversation; this also allows you to remain mysterious.

Another topic to avoid is talking about your future together. That includes taking her out in the future, or at the end of the date asking her out on a second date. If you start talking about your future together, you are basically going to lower your chances of having a future with her. You want the topic of a future together to be her idea. To talk about a future together communicates that you don't know how attraction works and that you are not very successful with women in general. Remember – you want her to be curious and unsure of her standing with you. If you tell her everything that's going to happen, there is no anticipation, no mystery, there is nothing to look forward to. You become boring and predictable. Women just want to show up for your date, look hot and follow your lead. Google "Corey Wayne 3 Ways To Seduce Women" for a detailed explanation on the 3 methods you can use to seduce women successfully. Make sure you click on the blue links in the text on my website articles for related articles and detailed techniques.

While you are on the date, you are going to be watching her for signs of growing attraction. Is she touching your hand? Is she touching your arm? Is she looking you in the eyes? One of the things you need to do is to look her in the eyes. Don't be looking around, looking at other women, or checking out other women. You need to be completely focused on her. Remember, sex must be the man's fault and it is your job to lead the date to a successful conclusion in the bedroom. Google "Corey Wayne Sex Must Be The Man's Fault."

When you look around and check out other women, she is going to think you are being a pig and that you are only out to get laid. As I said before, women like you more if they know you are popular with women. However, they want to feel more special than all the others you are dating. Your focus needs to be 100% on her having a good time, and finding out everything there is to know about your new lady. Otherwise, if she thinks you're just trying to get laid and will ditch her afterwards, she will reject you before you get the chance.

Another important point needing to be made is that women remember *everything*. They will remember where you went, what the restaurant was like, the people around you, and they will remember what they talked about. The color of the tablecloth, etc. *Listen up guys.* You need to really focus on the answers a woman is giving you to all the questions you are asking about her.

Make no mistake. You *will* be tested. She wants to know that you were really paying attention and cared about what she said. She will bring little things up here and there to test whether or not you were listening. If you pass those tests, it will definitely raise her attraction level, because now she knows you are interested in who she is. If you fail her test, she will keep testing you.

Dos and Don'ts of the First Date

- Don't spend the time talking about you. Do let her do most of the talking.

- Don't badmouth your ex-girlfriends or wives. Don't badmouth *her* ex-boyfriends or husbands, either. Do say positive things about your past relationships, or don't say anything at all.

- Don't overly compliment a woman, except maybe to tell her she looks nice when you pick her up or meet up, or that you had a good time at the end of a date. Most guys try to give ass-kissy compliments to get women into bed to the point it comes off as being phony or a clinical diagnosis. It comes off as a bribe for sex if you overdo it.

- Don't take her to extravagant places on the first date. If a guy starts spoiling a woman right away, she will come to expect that kind of treatment. Do take her someplace nice, quiet, intimate, and inexpensive, until you get to know her and know that she is really into you.

- Be careful talking about sex, even if she is the one to bring it up. Change the subject after a few playful sexual innuendos. Use it sparingly and then change the subject. Most guys just get themselves in trouble with this subject.

- Be a charming James Bond 90% of the time and 10% of the time a naughty little boy. Same thing with teasing. Treat her like a bratty little sister no more than 10% of the time or you will come off as just putting her down constantly.

- If she is pressing you about past relationships, don't give in to her pressing. Say, *I don't kiss and tell* with a James Bond playful smirk.

- Don't treat the service people badly. Many women have been involved in the service industry before in one capacity or another, and if they see you treating another individual in a demanding manner, they will often read that as a sign of the demanding individual you may become later in the relationship.

- Do tip your wait staff appropriately. Some guys will short change a wait person on tips. I have heard of women who will get embarrassed and slip extra money onto the table. It shows that you are cheap, and that you do not appreciate the things that others do for you.

The Secret of Dating

The whole experience of dating and discovering what you have planned in real time is what raises a woman's attraction to you. Her attraction to you increases based on how you ask her out when you call her on the phone and the anticipation of what is going to happen on a date. Don't call her and tell her everything you are going to do on the date, where you are going to go, what time you are going to do this and what time you are going to do that. Also don't ask her what she wants to do. Invite her to join you. You want it to be a surprise. You want it to be an unfolding of the evening. Be the leader and lead. The word lead means to go first.

So as the day approaches, she is now thinking about you, she is thinking about what she's going to wear, she is telling her friends, and she is looking forward to it. Since you have a definite date, it drives her crazy wondering if you are going to show up, what will happen, how it will go, etc. It creates excitement in her when you do. Remember, you are setting a date sometimes several days in advance. Most guys will call before they come and talk her out of going out with them.

I actually had one woman I went out with that wasn't ready when I showed up. When I asked her why she wasn't ready, she replied: *Honestly, I didn't think you were going to show up.* I said: *I told you that I'm a man of my word.* She proceeded to tell me that most guys call her before they come to pick her up. I was being completely different. It set me apart, because no guy has ever treated her that way before.

When you go to pick her up or meet up, you are a gentleman but not a doormat, you open the car door, and you take her to a fun place. Google "Corey Wayne Be A Gentleman, Not A Doormat." It is the experience of having the nice dinner, drinks, bowling, shooting pool, darts, great conversation, etc., and just having a good time. Whatever it is you are doing, for a woman the whole experience of the date is important. The less she knows, the more it heightens her anticipation and the more her attraction grows.

Do not make the mistake of thinking: *I took her to dinner, and great, now I'm ready to go home and have sex.* That is an attachment and expectation. Women don't operate that way. They warm up to you, and their hearts open a lot slower, because it is all about the whole emotional experience. You won't be able to sleep with every woman on the first date, but by the 2nd or 3rd on average. You have to practice. Google "Corey Wayne Hangout, Have Fun & Hook Up" for a detailed video and article on my website. Going to 2-3 different places in one evening can speed the process up as each place is like a date in and of itself. You can meet up for happy hour, then maybe go someplace for appetizers or dinner and then go shoot some pool or bowling, etc. Doing something physical and playful as the last place you go gives her the opportunity to start touching you. You can then make a move to kiss her and potentially take her back to your place or have her follow you there.

Don't waste your time with women that have a low level of attraction. Google "Corey Wayne The Myth Of The One" for a detailed article and video on my website you should read. *I can't stress this enough.* The higher her level of attraction, the easier she is going to make the date and the more fun both of you will have. In addition, you need to ask yourself this question: How many women have you taken out where you can't even remember their name? Dating can be an expensive proposition, the dollars add up quickly. Do you really want to spend all that money, and time, on a woman that isn't romantically attracted to you to begin with?

Again, when you are on the date, you will be a gentleman. You will hold doors open for her and open the car door. It's part of being a leader and leading the interaction to where you want it to go. When you walk down the street, you will take her hand to lead her across the street, but don't grab her hand and start holding it prematurely. As you are walking side by side her hand may start bumping yours, then you can take her hand. These are subtle things that cause her to start reaching out to you and start chasing you. If she's chasing you, she's not dumping you. It gives you all the power, which is what a woman wants anyway.

A lot of guys think: *Hey, I'm on a date. I can hold hands or put my arm around her.* Women will let you know when it is okay to touch. They will give you an invitation. The invitations are usually subtle, so again, you have to pay attention. When you are walking down the street, is she constantly bumping into you? Is she tapping your arm or brushing her hand on your arm when she is talking? If she has a really high level of attraction, she may even grab your hand and start holding hands with you, or put her arm around you. Then it's okay to reciprocate.

It is amazing to see, when I pay attention to these things, just how much women are telling you without words. It's all about her body language. I've had cases where I will be walking down the street with a woman, and we are on a big sidewalk. I will gradually start walking away from her, and she will either maintain the distance, or she will bump into me. If she is bumping into me that is a sign she wants to be touched. It's her signal to you that touching is okay. If she is working to maintain that space between you, then she has a lower level of attraction.

On one date with a woman, I was walking downtown on a wide street that had been closed to vehicle traffic for the evening for pedestrian traffic to the bars and restaurants. We were in the middle of the street, and since there was so much space, I just started slowly walking over to one side, away from my date. It was funny to see whether she would keep walking along with me. She didn't even notice it. I was pretty much walking all over the road, having fun with it. It shows that *she* was pursuing *me*, and that demonstrates high attraction.

Most of the time, she isn't even aware that she is doing this. Inside, you can be chuckling, because you are reading her attraction and know exactly where she is at. These are the types of things women will do. If she grabs your hand, then it is okay to hold hands with her. If she puts her arm around you, then it's okay to put your arm around her. The higher her attraction and the more comfortable she feels, the more she will start touching you. You need to let her give the invitation. It's always better that way and helps escalate things physically when she reaches out to you.

If she has her arm around you and then takes it away, you do the same until she gives you the next invitation. It is another subtle test women use to see if you are pursuing her more than she is pursuing you. When you have passed the test, she will eventually give you another invitation when it is okay to touch her again. Women are like cats that way.

All the while you are heading to your destination you will be keeping it funny and keeping it positive and uplifting. Joke around with her. She will probably ask you about previous women you have dated. She might ask if you are dating other women, or if you have been married. You want to give her an answer, but whatever the answer is; you want it to be positive. Positive topics elicit positive feelings. This creates attraction and causes her to associate feeling good with you.

As I mentioned before, too many guys decide to get all their baggage out on the table. You don't want to do this. Guys want to go on and on about all of their problems. On the date, she should be doing 70-80% of the talking. You want to ask questions. Women want to know that the guy is sincerely interested in who they are. They want to see that you want to know what they are all about.

A lot of guys, not only when they meet women, but when they are out on a date, or even when they call a woman on the phone to ask her out for a date, will either dump all their baggage on her, or will sit and talk about all of their accomplishments. Guys try to impress her. They try to do all these extravagant things, but only end up talking her out of liking them.

I don't have a problem with mentioning good things. But to discuss intimate details is not something a gentleman would do. Besides, the past is the past. It is between me and the woman in question. A gentleman doesn't go around telling intimate details of a relationship. A woman you have just met should accept and understand this. The chances are high that it will also make her feel more comfortable, because she can rest assured that you will treat any information she shares with you in the same manner.

Now she can feel more comfortable about opening up to you and sharing more personal things. She knows you will keep your mouth shut and not blab intimate details she may tell you to everyone you meet, especially your guy friends. Plus, the more you talk about her to your friends, the higher the likelihood is that it will get back to her and create problems for you.

While you are on your date, pay attention to what she is saying, but don't lean forward as though you are absorbing her presence. Lean back in your seat and be casual. Show her that you are confident and centered. Let her lean in toward you. Then you can invite her to sit next to you so you can get even closer. Lean back, spread your legs out and take up too much space like a king of his kingdom.

You should ask for the check and pay since you invited her out, signaling the end of the date without words. While you are doing this, watch for her reaction. Does she seem disappointed? Does she seem as though she could keep on talking, and is surprised by you ending the date so soon? These are all good signs that you have raised her attraction level even more.

The Kiss Test

At the end of the date, you are going to want to go for the goodnight kiss if you have not kissed her already. You want to kiss her on the lips and see if she kisses you back. If she is really interested in you, she will kiss you back.

If she turns her head and you get her cheek, it shows she doesn't have any romantic interest in you. At this point, you know that to go out with her again would be a waste of your time. One thing you don't want to do is to go in for the kiss, and try to kiss her on the cheek. A woman immediately takes this as a signal of your low attraction to her, or as a lack of self-confidence. A woman will read it as the "kiss of death", even though you might be trying to be a gentleman about it. Google "Corey Wayne Never Apologize For Wanting Her."

To give her a kiss on her lips shows confidence. It tells her: *I know I'm good enough for you. Here, let me show you.* You are showing her your strength and that you are totally in your masculine. Remember, women are designed to receive a man. It's up to you to be the leader.

All night long, you have found out everything about her, and she has found out little bits and pieces about you. You have shown your interest, while at the same time remaining a mystery to her. If this evolves into a long-term relationship, she has plenty of time to pull out information about you. By making her work to get to know you, you will remain mysterious and interesting. You'll also make sure she is sincerely into you.

After you give her a goodnight kiss, you are going to say: *I had a good time.* Or: *It was a nice evening.* Don't elaborate. Stay in your center, and leave her wondering just how good of a time you had. Make her think about whether everything went all right or not. She will replay the date over in her mind, looking back on all the clues. You are not giving her the answer. You are remaining a mystery. The whole time she is thinking about you and how the date went, her attraction level is going up.

Now you are going to leave. You are not going to tell her that you will call her. You are not going to set up the next date, or even talk about going out again. You are going to leave her wondering. It's a scientific fact that women are more attracted to men whose feelings are unclear. If you're not able to escalate things to more than just kissing, or you can tell it's going to take a few more dates for the Indoor Olympics to happen, it's time to go.

The same calling principle that I outlined previously applies to all dates for the first two months. So if you went out with her on a Thursday night, you won't call her until Monday or Tuesday to ask her out for your next date. It's better to always ask *when are you free to get together* when setting dates. This should remain consistent for the first two months. When you don't call her the next day after your date, she is going to wonder whether you liked her or not. If she is wondering about you, she will like you more. If her attraction goes up high enough, she may even actually call you. Again, you want her to start chasing you as soon as possible. This makes things so easy for you. Then you simply set the next date and get off the phone. Having a woman pursue you is the ideal place that you want to get to. There is no doubt in your mind at that point that her attraction is high.

The kiss test does not have to wait until the end of the date. If you are reading the signs of attraction correctly, you may find that she is signaling you earlier on in the date. I was on my first dinner date with one woman, and had been talking for hours. I was doing everything right with asking questions and letting her do 80-85% of the talking.

At one point she asked: *Can I give you a hug? You are so sweet and I am having such a good time.* I said: *Of, course.* We hugged, and two more times after that she asked me to hug her again. The second time, I sat back down and we started talking some more. She was leaning in really close, and at that point, her chair was right next to mine.

I just knew the time was right, and that she was ripe for it. I moved over and started kissing her. We were the only ones left in the restaurant, and we actually started making out right there. It was the fulfillment of the kiss test. I had built the anticipation so well at this point that she wanted to embrace me. She didn't actually kiss me, but the fact that she wanted to touch and hold me said that she was open to it. The invitation had been issued, so I didn't wait until the end of the date. Be the leader. Make it happen when the signs are there. Do not wait or hesitate. Men are direct and go for what they want.

Later she told me: *It really stunned me when you kissed me. I wasn't really ready for that. I was surprised and didn't like it at first.* I replied: *I could tell you didn't really like it, since you had your tongue in my mouth.* I didn't just kiss her, she was kissing me back. Again, a woman may say one thing, but her actions are saying something else. Google "Corey Wayne Pay Attention To What A Woman Does."

Here is another example to illustrate how easy it can be when a woman shows the right signs. Weddings are a great place to meet women. Everyone is happy and having a good time and the chances are if you find a woman you are interested in, that you will already know somebody that she knows.

I went to a wedding for a friend of mine from high school. I was 29 at the time, and his cousin, a beautiful redhead, was 18. During the rehearsal and rehearsal dinner she kept staring at me and checking me out.

The day of the wedding, at the reception, I walked over and started talking to her. She proceeded to tell me she had specifically asked one of her friends at the wedding for a pen and a piece of paper, so in the event that I asked, she could be prepared to give me her phone number and contact information, because she really liked me. We ended up hanging out, dancing, and having a good time. During the evening she was touching me, and at one point she was even sitting in my lap.

After that we went outside the reception hall and we sat down in the grass. We were talking, and she was sitting real close. I couldn't help myself. I had to kiss her. She had been giving all the signals of an invitation. She was pursuing me during the course of the evening, touching me, telling me she liked me, and even the fact that she had a high level of interest from the very beginning. This girl went out of her way to make everything easy for me.

The Right Approach

I was at a four-day retreat for personal growth, something that I am very passionate about. There were around fifty people there, all with the same focus. The first night I was checking everyone out to see what kind of people were there. I spotted a woman with dark hair, dark eyes, tan, a nice figure and a nice smile. I didn't think a whole lot about her at the time. I thought she was cute, even attractive, but it didn't hit me as a big deal.

The next afternoon at lunch, we were sitting at the same table, with one of her friends between us. We were talking, and got on the subject of movies. Her friend started telling me how she liked the *Lord of the Rings* movies, and we all went on talking about that. The woman I had noticed the day before started asking me all kinds of questions, joined the movie discussion, and my attraction actually started going up. I thought: *This girl is really charming. There's something about her. She has an energy that I just really like.*

So as we're talking, I start into my playful mode and start joking around and teasing her. We finished lunch and went back into the event. Later that evening, we all went to dinner together. I was being cocky, but she was also very confident in herself. She started talking about past relationships and men in her life. She told me about how guys would come and hit on her and how they came off very weak. There were stories about guys she had blown off and they never even realized what had happened. She was used to getting her way with guys, even the ones she dates, because no one stood up to her. She had a boyfriend by the way, but I still wanted to have some fun with her.

So she started asking me: *What do you do?* I told her: *I'm an author, a speaker, and most of what I do is to teach people how to reach their full potential. Right now I am working on a book to teach guys how to understand women.* She laughed and asked: ***You*** *are teaching guys how to understand women?*

Her tone was implying that I had no clue as to what I was talking about. It was all a test. I had been teasing her and being playful all day and then again all night at dinner. She sensed my confidence and cockiness, and she was testing to see if she could deflate me. I started teasing her and being even more playful. She started telling me that she didn't like me and said: *You aren't a very nice guy. You're mean.* She was being playful, but in a not-so playful way. She was trying to intimidate me. Google "Corey Wayne Women Bluff To Test Your Strength."

Everyone around us was having a good time and laughing at the interaction between the two of us. Here I was, sitting with a whole group of girls, and she was trying to make me look bad, as though I didn't know what I was talking about. So I started giving her a taste of the information I was working on, which was what I knew about understanding women. I explained the way things are with women, what motivates them, why they do what they do, and why guys do what they do.

As I start telling her what I knew about women, and explaining all of these things, over the course of about half an hour she went from a real hard core: *You don't know anything about women*, to: *I guess I was wrong. You really do know what you are talking about.* She had been testing me, and by staying centered and believing in who I was, she started to change her mind about me. After that she told me: *I didn't really like you at first, but you're actually a pretty cool guy.*

Beautiful women will often bluff you to test and see if you really are confident. Her bluff was in saying that she didn't like me, and it was her test to see if I would maintain my center, and be strong in who I was. I called her bluff, and some of her barbs had been pretty negative. She went from her telling me she didn't like me, to telling me she did, and after a couple glasses of wine she started saying: *Corey, I love you. You are so sweet.* This whole time she was touching me and moved her chair closer to me.

We sat there, continuing to talk. I kept my hands to myself, maintaining my composure, and leaning back in my chair. She was leaning forward and touching me. We all decided to go back to one of the girls' rooms. Each of us had these big Jacuzzis that could comfortably fit eight people.

So we start to walk toward the room, and we get about ten feet away from the dinner table and she grabs my hand and told me she wanted to hold it. I went back to my cabana and got changed, and we all ended up hanging out for a couple hours. All this time, we were talking, teasing, and joking back and forth.

On the third day of the event, she would come over and sit next to me. She would get up and leave with her friends once in a while but a little while later she would come back and sit next to me (remember the cat analogy?). At one point she said: *Let me crack your toes*. So she grabbed my toes and proceeded to crack them. It really hurt. I said: *Ow. That hurts*.

Later in the day, I was sitting outside the event on this low, three-foot wall, and she came over, grabbed my feet and started cracking my toes. It still really hurt. I got up and said: *Give me your hand*. She gives me her hand, smiling with a look that said: *What are you going to do now?* I lifted her hand up to spin her around, and as she spins, I spanked her on the butt in a playful, but firm way.

She turned around with a stunned look on her face and I just said: *Brat*. Then she tried to spank me back. I grabbed her hands and told her simply: *I'm the spank-or, not the spank-ee*. She said: *You can't spank me*. I told her: *Well, if you were not a brat, you wouldn't get spanked*.

I was being totally playful, and there was a shift that happened in her. I don't want guys to read this and think they can just simply get away with something like this. You can only get away with things like this if you totally own who you are. Don't just go out and grab the hands of women you meet and start spanking them. You have to be playful, but totally own your masculinity and be assured of what you are doing.

Later that night, which was the last night of the retreat, we were sitting in the Jacuzzi, talking again. At this point, there was another guy that came into the group (he would be considered a cock-blocker), and it was obvious he was also interested in this woman, as well as another one that was present. I was watching this guy continually going over to the one I spanked and touching her, and she was touching him back.

I maintained my composure and just sat there throwing little, funny remarks at her. She started telling me how she didn't like it. To show me just how much she didn't like it, she kept swimming over to where I was in the Jacuzzi, and proceeded to playfully slap or hit me. I would grab her and wrestle with her, dunking her under water.

Then she proceeded to tell her two girlfriends: *Corey spanked my ass yesterday. He can't do that.* They told her how they thought it was funny and playful. She was looking for them to gang up on me and bust my chops, which they didn't, because they really liked me, too.

Every few minutes she was away from me and would say something, and I would throw some funny little barb back at her. She would come back to my side of the Jacuzzi and start wrestling with me. One time I was over by where the seat was, and I pulled her up out of the water and spanked her bottom and pushed her back into the water.

Later she started again to tell me how she didn't like me, and so on. I looked right at her and said: *That's not true.* She turned to her friends for support and complained that I was doing this and that to her. Her two girlfriends basically said: *We haven't seen anything like this since we were in grade school. It's really fun to watch. It is obvious that you really like Corey.*

She replied: *I do not.* They said: *Yes, you do. Every five minutes you keep going over to him, wanting to play with him, touch him and wrestle with him. You wouldn't do that if you didn't like him.* This is the effect you can have on a woman when you are being playful, but still in your center.

Now, I want to be clear. She did have a boyfriend, so I didn't kiss her or anything. Why? It's just not the right thing to do. I was just playing with her and having fun. I simply won't mess with women who are married or who have boyfriends, but I will have some fun with them. Remember when I said you treat all women the same?

The point I am trying to make is that you should always be playful and open to meeting different women. One good thing to understand is that dating, courtship, and love should always be playful. You should always be having a good time with it. We didn't have any serious conversations. They were all humorous and fun. We were sharing stories and making each other laugh.

The next morning, when we were all saying our goodbyes, she came over, gave me a hug and said: Corey, *I had a lot of fun. I had a really good time with you.* That was it. If she had been single, I would have gone for the kiss, and later... given her the flesh rocket.

This also goes back to another point I mentioned earlier. Don't go into a relationship, any kind of relationship, with the thought of what you can get out of it. You should go into a relationship to give. This woman had a boyfriend. I knew that. I knew I wasn't going to get anything serious out of our time together, so I made it a fun experience for us both. That's how you need to approach all the relationships and women in your life. Always go into it to have fun, be playful, and just be a strong, confident, centered guy.

Part VII: Keep It Steady!

Continue the Mystery

From the beginning, I have talked about being a mystery to a woman. Let her do all the work of pulling the information out of you. This is so important, and I really wanted to emphasize that you need to maintain your level of mystery, not just in the beginning, but throughout the relationship.

So now you have been out on your first successful date. You have done everything right, and some people say: *Call her the next day and tell her what a wonderful time you had, just so she doesn't sit and wonder.* I say: *Wrong answer.* You **want** her to wonder about you, because again, that is going to have a positive effect on her attraction for you.

As far as timing, when do you call her? Let's say you have had your first date and everything went great. You are going to wait until the next week. You are going to use the same principle you used when you called her for the first date. In the beginning you date once a week until she starts initiating contact and reaching out to you first. Once she starts reaching out to you several times a week you'll simply set the next date and get off the phone.

You're the leader who starts the dating process by going out once per week, and she escalates the frequency of dates by her calling you a day or two later and you setting the next date. As her attraction grows she calls you more and more. Therefore, you start to see each other more and more. If she ever backs off, always go back to the once per week rule where you initiate one phone call per week to set one date per week.

If you had your date with her Wednesday or Thursday, you are going to call her the following Monday or Tuesday to ask her out for a date by saying, *when are you free to get together?* The important thing is that you want to limit your dates to once a week until she starts calling or texting you after dates. Then you use her initiated contact to set the next date. When you make your date, set it up a couple days in advance.

The goal is to get her to start reaching out to you first, and then you set the next date and get off the phone. This is what causes her to start chasing you. Google "Corey Wayne Texting That Attracts Vs. Repels." It always shows more confidence and masculinity if you call instead of texting her. However, if she texts you first, it's okay to use texting to set the next date. Assume if she contacts you that she wants to see you. Therefore, make a date happen in as few steps as possible.

This is similar to the concept of spoon-feeding her your time. When you are not with her, then she is thinking and wondering about you and this increases her attraction to you.

If *she* calls *you* to talk, that is her way of saying: *I like you. I'm trying to get your attention.* That's what women do. The more they like you, the more they want your attention. The more they want your presence.

Typically what happens is after the 2nd or 3rd date she starts texting or calling you a day or two later. Then the 2nd or 3rd week you will start seeing her about twice a week because she's reaching out to you more and more. By week 5 or 6 you will be seeing each other about 3 times per week. By week 7 she should be starting to fall in love and starting to bring up the topic of being exclusive. Google "Corey Wayne How To Keep A Relationship Casual When She Wants To Be Serious."

The Pursuit

If she does happen to call you, remember: The phone is for making dates, not being her therapist, emotional tampon or gay male girlfriend. You need to maintain the attitude of a busy guy. You will say: *Hey, what's going on?* She may say: *Oh, I just wanted to tell you that I had such a great time the other night at dinner, and just wanted you to know I was thinking about you.* These are good signs. The fact that she has called you means that she is now pursuing you, which is a great thing. It means that you did a good job on your first date.

Not all women are going to call you after the first date. Actually, very few of them will, except the ones that have an extremely high attraction for you to start with. If they do call you, you can say something along the lines of: *Great. Well, I had a really nice time, too. When are you free to get together next?* She: *I'm free Sunday and Tuesday.* You: *Great. How about Sunday, blah, blah, blah?* She: *Okay* Make definite plans to meet up or pick her up.

The goal is to eventually get the woman to start pursuing you. If she's pursuing you, it means she really likes you. But if she hasn't called and you went out on a Monday, you are going to wait until the following week to call her, and again ask her when she is free.

If you do everything right for the first two months, she will be in love with you by the end of the second month. By week 7 or 8 she will be calling or texting you 2-3 times a day and you will pretty much be together all of the time.

Regardless, for the first two months, the phone is for setting appointments, *period*. It is *not* for getting to know her. Sales people sell you in person, not over the phone. If you give away all the information about yourself over the phone, it makes you boring and predictable. You are not being centered.

All of the sudden, you will see yourself going from a guy that has been really busy, maybe dating ten other women, to a guy that has nothing else going on. A few weeks into the relationship, if you start doing that, she will *stop* pursuing you. Google "Corey Wayne Why Chasing Women Guarantees Rejection" and "Corey Wayne Excessive Contact Causes Rejection." You will start pursuing her again and she won't be as eager to see you. This is because you have actually been turning her off. She's getting bored because you are acting like a woman, not a man. Google "Corey Wayne Women Need To Wonder About You."

So it's a dance. It's more of an art than a science. It is a balance, and you have to understand that you *always* have to read her level of attraction. This is an important concept: *If she is always chasing you, then she's not dumping you.* She can't be breaking up with you, if *she* is pursuing *you*.

If she is calling you all the time, keep the conversation short. Tell her you are really busy, but you really would like to see her and ask her when she is free to meet up. Make it a definite date. Don't let her try and give you the: *Call back to confirm.* She will respond: *Great.*

Initially, in the first month or two of dating, you haven't built an emotional bond with her yet. Google "Corey Wayne You've Got

Nothing To Prove To Women." You are kind of on probation in her eyes. She is slowly opening up to you emotionally, as long as you continue to pass her tests and do things right. Over the long term, once you have started to successfully open her up emotionally to you, because of your strength, she will continue to open up more and more. She will want more and more of your presence, time and who you are as a man.

What usually happens to me is that the first couple weeks, I will be the one that calls and asks her out on a date. As she gets comfortable, her attraction level starts to get to a 7, or an 8. Then she will actually start calling me. When she calls, I ask her out for the next date.

Just remember: *Until she is in love with you, you want to stay off the phone, even if she is calling you.* When she calls you, take the opportunity to make the next date with her. If you are letting her come to you by setting dates when she contacts you, you'll never have to worry about over pursuing and turning her off. Google "Corey Wayne Let Women Come To You."

The important concept to grasp is the need to back off. In my situation, I had met a woman I really liked. We started dating. At one point, she started calling me all the time. I always answered her phone calls and was always available. We started seeing each other a lot. Suddenly, without my paying attention to the signs, she was starting to tell me: *I'll call you when I'm on my way*, and giving me other types of wishy-washy responses.

What happened is I was no longer making definite plans, and was placing myself at her beck and call. Without realizing it, I was slipping into that mode where I thought: *Okay. We've been dating long enough and I can just hang back a little. No big deal.* We started talking on the phone more and more and seeing each other in person less and less.

The end result was eventually she reached the point where she called and said: *I'll call you when I'm on my way*, I replied: *No problem.* We never set a definite time, and I went along with it. Then she started telling me some wishy-washy nonsense about her cousin wanting her to come over, and I said: *We have a date tonight. I'm here waiting for you.* At that point she canceled on me and I didn't hear from her for several days.

What happened was that I was allowing her to totally have her way with me. She would make plans when she wanted to make plans, and call me when she wanted to call me. My being at her beck and call was being weak. She was no longer curious. At that point, she knew she could have me.

I wasn't paying attention to her attraction level. She wasn't in love with me, so it was way too soon for me to do the things I did in this situation. What I want you to understand is that if you screw up, let's say you are dating and she's calling every day and then all of the sudden she backs off, don't call her because she didn't call you. Nine times out of ten, it's a test. You need to hang back and wait. Go back to the once a week rule.

If you are talking to her every day and then the last time you hear from her is on a Wednesday, don't call her until the following Monday or Tuesday to ask her out for a date. Make sure it is a definite date. If she won't give you a definite date, do the take away. If she responds with: *Okay. We'll do it some other time*, wait until the following week to call and ask her out again. If you still can't make a definite date with her, don't bother calling to ask her out again, because at that point, for whatever reason, her attraction has dropped too far. Remember: *If she likes you, she will help you.* Pay attention, and don't get sloppy.

Another example I can give involves a friend of mine. He had met a woman he really liked. When he first met her, he made it very clear that he liked her. He was talking about taking her out on a date, and was able to get her phone number.

He called her the next day and got her voice mail, and she never returned his call. A few days later, he called her again. Now to explain this a little better, she gave him her cell phone number. I asked: *When you called did it go straight to voice mail?* He told me: *Each time I called, it would keep ringing and then finally go to voice mail.* I told him: *Okay. It's on her cell phone. You left two messages, which you know she has received. She obviously has her cell phone on, and knows when she has missed calls. Don't call her again. You've left two messages, if she's interested, she will call you back. If you keep calling her, she is going to see you as weak and needy, and she will definitely not return your calls. You already did a sloppy job when you first met her.*

At this point, the only thing for him to do was to walk away. So he didn't call her. A week went by and he really wanted to call her to find out what had happened. I told him: *Just hang back. She will either call you, or she won't. If she doesn't, it's because you came off as too weak when you met her.* Over two weeks went by before he came to me and said: *Corey, you're not going to believe what happened.* I said: *Hmmm... let me guess. She called you?*

He replied: *Yes.* I asked: *Did you make a definite date?* He said: *Yes. We're going out on Thursday.* I told him: *Good job.* I had coached him what to do if she did call. Don't talk on the phone for an hour, it will lower your mystery and reduce the anticipation. Make a definite date, get her address, and tell her you are going to pick her up; or give her the place or address of where you want to meet her. Mention that you are busy, but you look forward to seeing her and get off the phone. He went out with her, and they've been together for over eight months now.

Had he continued to call and pursue her, she most likely would have never gone out with him. He would have completely missed his opportunity. It was over two weeks before she finally called him back. The bottom line is that if she is interested in you, she is going to call you. Don't start running after her. Like the cat, you will only chase her away. Google "Corey Wayne Women Are Like Cats, Men... Dogs."

All women, whether you are just starting to date or you have been together for a long period of time, will test you by not calling you. Even if she is totally pursuing you and calling you every day, at some point, she will test you by not calling. Don't run after her, especially if this happens within the first two months. Wait until the following week to call her, set a definite date and get off the phone.

If she is someone you have been dating and are in a serious relationship with and she stops calling, you also need to let this go. Call her up the next week. Obviously she is upset about something if she goes from calling and texting you 2-3 times a day for several months and then stops calling you suddenly. Be indifferent and say: *Hey. How are things going?* Sometimes women will stop calling to test you. If things are too easy and just going along, she will back off on purpose to see if you run after her. Stand your ground. You can't react to the fact that she has all of the sudden stopped calling you. If you do, she will see you as being needy and back off even more.

If a woman calls you in those early days of dating and has something she wants to talk about, just tell her: *Honey, I want to hear everything about it. Why don't you tell me all about it when I see you tomorrow night,* or: *Tell me all about it when I see you on Tuesday. I want to hear about it all then. That way I can give you 100% of my attention. I'm really jammed up right now and can't talk.*

Stay off the phone until she is completely head over heels in love with you. By staying off the phone, you are limiting your contact with her. It builds anticipation and lowers your chances of talking her right out of liking you. While she is waiting for the day to come when she gets to see you again, her attraction level is going up. Once it gets to a 9 and she is completely head over heels in love with you, she is going to be calling you all the time anyway. She will start calling you every day.

Only then you can loosen up a little bit, but keep in mind that the phone can make things boring and predictable. Some guys get hung up on: *Oh, I'm having this great conversation with this girl,* but they never go out on dates with her. Unless you're going out on dates, sleeping together, etc., you don't have a romantic relationship. You are only friends. Google "Corey Wayne How To Turn A Friend Into A Girlfriend."

Moving Into Relationships

How do you know when it's time to go steady? When she is emotionally ready, usually by week 7 of dating she will bring it up. Until then, hangout, have fun and hook up. Rinse. Recycle. Repeat. You just gently lead, so she *thinks* it's her idea.

She'll let you know when she wants to go steady. Keep dating other women until she tells you she wants to be exclusive, or until she does not want you to date any other women because she's not dating anyone else. Remember: When she brings up the topic, don't assume she wants to be exclusive. Ask her, *what do you mean*? If she says, *where is this going?*

Put who you are out into the world and accept whatever comes back. If you love any other way, it is attached, needy love. Real love is none of these things.

I wanted to give you an example of how it looks when a woman basically says: *I only want to date you.* I was dating a girl several years ago that I really liked. I was also still dating other women. She knew I was dating other women – she was dating other guys, too.

It came to a point where we were seeing a lot of each other. We had been dating for a couple months, and we were seeing each other two to three times a week. We were driving in the car one day and she said: *I know you have these other girls you are friends with that you also date.* Then she jokingly added: *But you'd better not be sleeping with any of them.* That was one way for her to tell me *I want you all to myself* and that she wanted to be exclusive.

Later on in the same conversation she said: *I know you have a lot of other women that are friends, and you've dated a lot of different girls, but if I found out you were still dating other women, I'd be really upset.* After my asking the "what do you mean?" question, she finally came right out and said: *I don't want you to be dating anybody else. I want you to be dating only me.* I responded by saying: *What do you mean? Are you saying I have to get rid of all these other girls?*

She replied: *Yes.* I answered: *Well, can I keep just one of them?* At this point, I'm teasing of course, I'm being playful about it. She said: *No.* I asked: *Does that mean I have to burn my little black book, too?* She said: *Yes.* I said: *What if I keep a photocopy, just in case?* She said: *Nope. You have to get rid of your book.*

She was laughing the whole time we were saying this, but this was how she came out and said: *I want you and I to be exclusive. This is what I want.* Never forget, even when you are moving into more serious topics in your relationship, love is playful. Keep it funny and positive, even with serious subjects. Don't get into a serious discussion thinking you have to do things a certain way. Love is supposed to be fun.

Don't talk about your future, because you will lower your chances of being in it. Let her be the one to bring it up. You need to make it her idea. It's like that in nature. You see a lot of animals competing for a female, and she decides which male she's actually going to mate with, who is suitable, and who is acceptable to her. It's the same thing with men and women. Women are going to decide who they want to date exclusively, and who they don't.

Remember: *The couple that plays together stays together.* Think of it as though you are two children, always wanting to have fun. That is the approach you need to take with your relationships to keep the magic alive long-term.

A guy that understands these principles doesn't need to ask where a woman is as far as her interest is concerned, or where the relationship is going. He would be acting like a woman if he did. He always knows where her attraction level is. He is always going to judge a woman by what she does. Most guys don't really understand what the meanings of her words are.

Testing During the First 60 Days

Let's say a woman breaks a date with you. Your relationship has been going along well and all the sudden she starts breaking dates. Right after she has broken the date, she says: *But I can't wait to see you again.* Men scratch their heads in confusion, thinking: *What does that mean?* If she really wanted to see you – guess what? You'd be going out with her. You would be spending time with her. You have to understand what the meanings of the words are. Guys tend to project their attraction and assume it's mutual.

Another thing that's really important to remember is that if a woman shares information with you, you always want to remember it. If a woman goes out on a date with you, she will remember the color of the tablecloth. She can tell you what outfit she were wearing, what you had for dinner, what she had for dinner, and what the bottle of wine was – she remembers everything. Once again, you are left scratching your head, thinking: *What?* You will be tested later to see if you were really listening.

It may be two or three dates down the road, but she is eventually going to say: *Oh, remember when we were talking about this, and remember when I told you that story?* If your response is: *No, I've never heard that story*, she is going to know that you weren't listening to her. That goes over like a lead balloon.

So when you are looking her in the eyes and acknowledging this stuff, you have to remember, because there **will** be a test later. If you fail that test, then she will start throwing other things at you to see if you were listening *that* time. You will start hearing those age-old words: *You don't listen to me.* And you will give the age-old response: *Yes, I do.* When a woman says you are not listening to her, she is indicating that you are not remembering the things she's saying, or understanding where she's coming from. Google "Corey Wayne How To Communicate With Women Effectively."

In her mind, you are *not* listening to her. You may be *looking* at her, but are you *hearing* what she is saying? Are you *remembering* everything she is saying? Granted, we may not remember things as well as women do, but you had better start remembering the gist of the conversation. It will make her feel hurt and create unnecessary drama.

Women are always going to push to see what your boundaries are. They might say things playfully when they're dating: *If you don't do this for me, I'm not going to see you any more.* My ex-girlfriend from London would tease me and say: *Well, I'm not going to come see you, then. I'm not going to come see you next month,* or: *I'm not going to come see you in a few weeks.*

I would respond: *Okay. Well, I guess it's time to get out the old black book and call up some of my old girlfriends, then.* She said: *You don't have a black book.* I replied: *Yes, I do. I just hid it in a very safe place.* She said: *Well, I'm not going to come see you.* I answered: *Okay. You're not going to come see me. I'm sorry for all the fun that you're going to miss out on. I guess I'll just have to spend my time with somebody else.*

I would just banter and be playful. It was her way of testing, because guys will bite into that, and say: *What do you mean you're not going to come see me?* She then replies: *Oh, I'm thinking about not coming. I have a lot of things going on.* Him: *But I really want to see you.* Her: *Well, that's really sweet, but, you know...* It's her way of testing to see: *Are you really strong?*

In this situation, she wanted to know that if she didn't come, I would still be myself without her being there. She was trying to test and see how badly I really wanted her to come see me. Her tone was serious when she called, almost as if to say: *Hey, something might be coming up.* I took on an attitude of being jokingly indifferent in this case.

She was bluffing to test and see where she stood. She did come to see me, and later when we were driving back from the airport, she said: *Were you worried that I wasn't going to come?* I gave her a joking glance and replied: *No. I knew you were going to come. I knew the only reason you threw that out there at all was to test to see if you could get a rise out of me. I never doubted you were going to come.* She broke down and laughed so hard. She admitted that I was right. The whole thing had been a test, and she was just teasing and playing around to see if she could get a reaction. She was bluffing to test my strength.

Again, women will always test you. If things have been going well, she will test to stir things up. She will do it just to make life interesting and to break up the monotony. Any time a woman senses a weakness, she is going to test you and exploit it more. If she senses you are needy, or maybe she said something that made you jealous then she is going to do more of what made you jealous. She is going to do more of what made you feel needy, just to make sure you really **aren't** needy. The more she senses the weakness, the more she's going to push, and the more she's going to test.

You have to become comfortable with being yourself. You need to make it part of who you are. Sooner or later, you will own it. And you *have* to own it, because if you can't maintain it later in the relationship, if you ever let that down, you are not the person she thought you were in the first place. She will see weakness and test and pull away, which makes you start to pursue, and that will drive her away even more.

You have to be strong and in your center. You need to be indifferent and walk away, if necessary. A woman has to know that if she pushes you too far, you will walk and never look back. The strongest negotiating position is being able to walk away and mean it. Until she knows and feels that, you are never going to completely own her heart.

The Big Bounce

I want to talk for a moment about backing up when things start to get squirrelly. What happens if you have been seeing a woman consistently and now she doesn't seem to get excited about seeing you, or you can tell her attraction is dropping? You always want to be aware of that. What is happening is the anticipation is not where it needs to be, and you are not being mysterious and unpredictable enough.

It is time to pull back a little bit. Back up. If normally you call her back right away when she calls you, wait an hour or two. If you always answer the phone when she calls, let it go to voice mail. It is taking two steps forward, one step back. Women pull away, they bluff, and they test. The more you chase after them, the more they run away and the more they test. Remember, the ideal place to be in a relationship is with the woman pursuing you. Back up and let her find the thrill of the chase again. Guys should never call or pursue more than 20-30% of the time. Any time a guy does more than 30%, the woman slowly loses attraction.

When dating a woman who has just come out of a long-term relationship or marriage, you have to keep in mind that her feelings are going to be really raw. Emotional healing takes time.

I had one girlfriend that I was really good friends with. I used to do an infomercial in Orlando and she was my co-host. I could tell there was chemistry between us. I actually took her out, because all the signs of high attraction were there. We had a lot in common, and our resumes were almost identical.

We went out the first and second week. When I called the third week to ask her out, all of the sudden I was getting real wishy-washy answers. Everything seemed as though it had been going great, and her attraction level was going up. The week before when we were kissing, she almost sucked the tongue out of my mouth and had invited me into her apartment at the end of our date. I later found out she had started seeing a guy she had dated for about two years. She had broken up with him about six months before, and then got back together with him. That's what had happened.

Keep in mind that the emotions of women who are on the rebound are very raw, and they may display very high levels of attraction. You could go out and have a great date and all of the sudden they don't ever want to see you again. They can't see you any more, and you are left scratching your head again: *Why? What happened?* They weren't emotionally ready yet. That's all it takes.

One other important point for avoiding the big bounce is: *Don't try to make your girlfriend, your wife, or your lady your mama or therapist.* If you've had something hard to deal with in your life emotionally, or are dealing with emotional baggage, don't cry every night in your woman's arms. It might be okay the first night, but if it's an on-going thing, and you are looking for someone to take care of and baby you, it is one of the quickest ways to turn your lady off. Why? You're simply acting like a woman. You MUST be the leader. Save your sad stories and insecurities for you best buddies.

If you are looking for a woman that is *that* giving, you are looking for someone that is totally in her feminine energy. If that's where she is at, she isn't going to want to deal with your neediness. A woman in her full feminine wants a man that's in his full masculine. She wants a strong, centered, confident guy.

The "L" Word

When I tell a woman that I love her, I usually let her say it to me first. When she is ready, she will come right out and say it. Most guys, on the first date or the second date, are already saying: *I love you.* Women respond by pushing that neediness away: *What? I don't even know you yet.*

As I said before, guys are visual for the most part. Guys fall in love through their eyes and women through their ears. Men go instantly to that place of: *Oh, wow, I'm going to marry her.* Women take longer. Women go out on first dates with the attitude of let's just see what happens.

How this usually unfolds is that you start dating her, and you have the first two months of the relationship. You are going out with her once a week. Somewhere around week 7 she will move into the: *I love you* phase. If you do everything right, she will be head over heels in love with you after two months or week 8. The more you screw up, the longer it will take for her to fall in love.

As you get toward the end of those two months and she has said those magic words: *I love you*, you should have already seen it coming. By now, you should have known exactly where her attraction was, because you have been watching for the signs every step of the way.

Some women may have a harder time saying the actual words. But again, you will have been watching for all the signs. You will know when she has reached that level. If she's calling you all the time, calling you once or twice a day: *I can't wait to see you again. I miss you so much.* That tells you exactly where she's at. *I'm dying to see you. I had such a great time the other night. When can I see you again?* It is her way of saying: *Hey, I'm wide open to whatever you want.* She is telling you: *I want your attention. I want all of your presence.*

If you follow the script of just setting the next date when she reaches out to you, you'll pretty much be together all the time by week 7 or 8. If she's totally in love with you, she is going to be calling you all the time, anyway. That way you never have to worry about pushing things along too fast. Since she's reaching out to you, you'll be spending more time together at her pace. She opens up to receive you more and more as her attraction level rises.

You won't even have to call her any more once she starts calling and texting you several times a week. When she does call you to talk, you just make your date on the phone and say: *Great. Tell me all about it when we go to dinner, etc.* It will make her anticipate spending time with you: *Oh, I can't wait to see him.* When you finally pick her up and go out, she can just completely unload all this stuff she has wanted to share with you. You will be able to see how excited she is to see you. You will be able to feel it when she showers you with her affection and love. It's a lot more fun that way and it makes things really easy and simple for you.

Part VIII: Solving the Mystery

Pay Attention!

Paying attention is, simply put, just being aware. It is important to always use the chart we demonstrated in Part V as your little radar. Once you have passed the first two months of dating, you are going steady with your girlfriend and everything is going well, paying attention becomes an important part of maintaining what you have worked so hard for.

You are still going to always be judging her level of attraction. You are always going to be watching what she does. You are always going to be watching her actions. Otherwise, it is too easy to slip into complacency. I still do this. You start not paying attention, or you don't call. You don't take your lady out. You don't do what you should. She will subtly let you know. By the time you figure it out, her attraction level has dropped beyond possibility of salvage, and she is gone from your life.

I had a girlfriend once that I had been dating for about six months. I was getting complacent. I wasn't sure that I really wanted to stay in the relationship. I was having a lot of doubts.

She had this guy she dated before me and had blown off when we first met. I remember one night we had talked on the phone, and I was kind of short with her. I was real busy. I honestly didn't even realize it. I was just really stressed out from work. She usually called me two or three times a day. Over four days went by and I hadn't heard from her. I thought: *Uh-oh. I must have done something to really piss her off.*

So I called her, and she told me: *I went out with my **friend**,* (meaning her ex) *and he told me I shouldn't break up with you. He was holding my hand and comforting me. He said I should make it work with you.* I thought the whole reason she was telling me this was to say: *Hey dude, this is your replacement. If you don't get your act together, I already have your replacement lined up.*

When she told me this it was the beginning of the end for me. I never felt comfortable trusting her again. She was telling me she wanted to get married a few weeks before, and after only one slipup she was hanging out with backup. Not cool.

You have to be able to read between the lines. This was her subtle way of saying: *You are really screwing up here.* Women won't lie. They will always tell you what is going on. If your relationship isn't going well, or **you** think it's going well, and she starts telling you about this really nice guy that she works with, who has been asking her out and hitting on her, and he's really nice... If she is talking about this other guy positively, it is her way of saying: *You need to wake up and get with the program. I have somebody else that's interested in me. If you keep turning me off, you are going to get replaced.*

Women are not going to come right out and say it. They are a lot more subtle and you have to learn to read between the lines. If you are screwing up and are not spending the time with her that you should, or you are not treating her like you should, you can always tell by how she is acting toward you. Has she stopped lovemaking, kissing, and is no longer touching you? Does she not seem as happy to see you any more? Maybe she's a little bitchy when you get home? Google "Corey Wayne Beware Of The Bitchy Woman."

This is all her way of saying: *You are failing at making me happy. You are failing at giving me your presence and your love, and so therefore, I'm shutting down.* A lot of guys will say: *She's just being a bitch.* But it is her way of saying that *you* are being weak, and *you* are not being centered, and *you* are not taking care of business the way *you* should be.

Once you have passed the first few months and your lady is totally in love with you, the more of your presence and love you give your lady, the more she wants from you. Women are all about opening up and receiving your love and your presence. The masculine energy is all about purpose, drive, direction, and mission in life, and breaking through barriers.

Physically, women open up and receive. They are penetrated in every way by their man. And men, in every way, penetrate the world and their woman. So the more you give to your lady, the more she wants from you. That is why she calls you during the day: *Hey, just calling to see what you're doing.* It's like a big billboard saying: *Hey, I just want to feel your love, I want to feel your presence.* That's why, when you walk in the door, she doesn't even have to tell you she loves you. She runs up to you and puts her arms around you and kisses you. It is because she wants to feel the love that you have for her.

It is also why, when she says: *Hey, look, I had my nails done today.* If you say: *Honey, I'm watching TV,* this is the **worst** thing you can do. You are basically saying to her: *I don't love you. I'm not giving you any of my presence. Get the hell out of my way. You are unimportant to me right now.* You are invalidating what is important to her.

When she says: *I just had my hair done. What do you think, honey?* You have to stop what you are doing, and say: *You look beautiful. You look great... she did a great job. I love your nails... I love that new dress you just bought. Your new hair color looks great. That new handbag? I think it goes great with that outfit. You look really hot.*

Women **want** to be noticed. Everything they do is about getting your attention. That is why it's so important to understand what your attention means to them.

One of my friends wrote a testimonial saying that I saved his relationship. His girlfriend was doing everything she could to try and get his attention. All she wanted to do was *feel* him. I told him: *Your sole purpose for being in that relationship is to give to her. So you either need to give to her or go out and get yourself a hooker. Then you can have a transactional-based relationship with no emotional attachments. It's horse-trading in essence.*

Once he got that, he understood that everything she was doing – the clothes she was wearing, and the hair – was all about her saying: *I want to feel your love. I want to feel your presence.*

Basically, what happens is that without your presence, a woman closes down. She shuts down and puts a wall up. You have shut her down because you haven't given her your presence. So she is going to make it ten times as difficult for you to get back into her heart again. She is going to test you and make it really hard, because she wants to be sure that if she *does* open up to receive your love that you are going to give that love and presence to her.

If you tell her you love her, and you don't show by your actions that you love her it's just an: *Oh, I love you.* It means nothing to her if you are not still romancing her. In her mind, if you really *did* love her, you would be *showing* her that you loved her. If you really *did* love her, you would spend the time trying to find out what is bothering her. You would *want* to know what's really upsetting her. You would get to the root issue, and let her communicate so she feels like you completely understand her. Google "Corey Wayne How To Communicate With Women Effectively."

So, what happens is that there is a shift. Once you have passed her test and proven you *are* worthy, it is an on-going process. As long as you continue to do things right, she will remain open to you, and if she ever *does* shut down on you, then it is your job to break through those barriers. When you have time in with her and been with her for a while, it's a lot easier to do that, as opposed to when you first met her.

So that's why a woman is going to call you in the middle of the day and say: *Hey, I just wanted to call and tell you that I love you.* All she's looking for is to feel you. She wants to feel your presence. She wants to know that you love her and you care about her. But when you are really busy at work, you can't stop what you are doing, just talk to her every time she calls. Google "Corey Wayne Why Women Prefer To Chase Men."

Here is a good example: One of my former business associates is a very weak guy, and his wife is extremely needy. She used to call him three or four times a day because she was so insecure. He had cheated on her two or three times over the course of their marriage, and they had been together for about 15 years. When she constantly called him, what she was looking for without realizing it, was validation: *Does he still love me? Is he still being faithful to me?* That was something he had fallen down on a few years earlier in their marriage. So her fear was real.

No matter what it was, he would stop whatever we were doing to sit there and talk to her. Once we were in a meeting with about ten people and she just kept calling over and over again, because he wouldn't pick up. Finally, he started to worry that it was an emergency. He picked up the phone and said: *We're in a meeting, are you okay? Is there an emergency?* She said: *Oh, no. I just wanted to call and see how you were doing.* He replied: *I'm in a meeting. That's why I kept sending you to voice mail. The only reason I answered was because you kept calling back and I thought there was something wrong.*

If your wife or girlfriend calls you in the middle of the day and you are busy doing something, you should not stop what you're doing just to talk to her. What you should do, if you answer the phone and are talking to her, is say: *Honey, I'm really busy. It was really sweet of you to call and tell me how much you care. I just want you to know that I appreciate the phone call. I can't talk right now, but I'll definitely see you tonight.*

When you go home that night, **show** her how much you appreciated her calling: *It was good hearing from you today. I love hearing your sweet voice in the middle of the day.* While you were at work, you weren't really able to talk to her. She may have felt a little rejected, like you couldn't make time for her, but you just happened to be busy focusing on your purpose. She may be feeling a little down about that, so this is your opportunity to really open her up and acknowledge what she did. It was her way of saying: *I just want you to know that I love you by calling in the middle of the day.*

Acknowledge it. Kiss her, hug her, and say: *It was really good hearing for you. I just love hearing your voice.* That's all you have to say. It makes her feel as though: *He really does care.* Again, pay attention. Women want your attention all the time. You have to acknowledge the things they do to get your attention.

Acknowledge everything they do, because you are the one who opened them up, and you worked hard at always building anticipation. Now they are always looking at receiving your love and receiving your presence. That's what the purpose is to her phone calls during the day, the e-mails, why they write you little cards, why they leave you little notes, and go shopping. It is why they spend two to three hours at the salon getting their hair done. They are just a big billboard that's saying: *Show me how much you adore me, and worship me, and love me.*

When you first come home from work, it is important that the first thing you do before anything else is to go up to your wife and say: *Hey, honey, how was your day?* If she jumps in your arms and is hugging and kissing you, it tells you her attraction is a 9 and everything is great. If she says: *I had a horrible day,* guys have to understand that your lady doesn't want you to solve her problems. She just needs you to listen to them. If you are unsure when she starts talking say, *do you want my advice or do you just want me to listen?*

So say to her: *Well, tell me about your day…* It is important to have specifics in there and say things like: *How'd that make you feel?* And: *Don't leave anything out.* What I will often do is while she talks on and on, I'll say: *Well, what else? Tell me more.*

You are pulling out everything that happened, because just by talking about it, it creates rapport. It is making her feel better just by saying: *So if I understand you right, you were talking to your girlfriend Sally, and this, this, and this happened, and she said that, and it made you feel this way.* Repeat back some of what she said to you. It is your way of acknowledging her and letting her know that you understand her, because women want to be understood.

The Art of Communication

One of the clients I am coaching was in a meeting with his girlfriend the other day. Besides being in a relationship, they also work together. Whatever he said in the meeting, it was as though she was countering everything. She was disagreeing with everything he was saying. I told him: *The reason why she is disagreeing with you is because things are not going well between the two of you.*

The reason she is so against, or adamantly opposing him is that he was being weak. He failed in his mission and his purpose. This was her way of kicking him in the knees and getting him to step up, be a man, and stand up to her. She was testing him and using this as an opportunity to try out a confrontation with him.

She was throwing a storm at him, and she wanted him to stay present and strong. What I suggested in this situation was to acknowledge what she was saying: *I appreciate the fact that you said this, this, and this, and I appreciate your input. However, you have only been working with me for a few months. I have had this business for many years, and this is what works. This is what my decision is.*

She was still really nasty, and would throw barbs at him. He finally turned to her and said: *I am in a really good mood today, and I'm going to stay in that mood. I have things I have to do, so I'm going to go*. And he left. She had been doing this in front of some other employees, and had been way out of line. I told him: *You absolutely did the right thing there*.

If he had sat there and tried to argue with her, all it would have accomplished was to have it escalate into a big argument in front of everybody in the office. He was centered. He was strong. He was not letting her get to him. That was what he needed to do in that case.

As I explained to him, nine times out of ten, if she's mad at you for not taking out the garbage, you take the garbage out and she's still angry at you, then it's not that she was mad at you about the garbage. The reason she was angry was that you gave her your word and then didn't keep it. When a guy does that, it does not make his lady feel safe. It makes her doubt his masculine core. When she doubts his core, she either has to test him to feel his strength, or to help get him to step up and be a stronger man. You should read David Deida's *"The Way of The Superior Man."*

One of the things I use a lot to break tension is humor. If I have done something that has really made my girlfriend mad, I will try to be humorous about it. I'll tease her. I'll banter back and forth just to get her to loosen up and to get her back into her feminine and to where she can be playful again. It is very important to use humor and be playful, and not take things seriously. I'm being the leader. I'm setting the tone. I'm choosing not to have or create any drama in my life.

That's why communication is so important. If she has shut down and you say: *What's wrong, honey?* She'll say: *Oh nothing. Everything's just fine.* If you say: *Okay. As long as everything's fine*, and then you go sit down in front of the television. She may come out and say: *Why don't you take the damn garbage out?* She's not mad at you for not taking the garbage out. She is angry because you haven't opened her back up. For some reason she's not trusting your masculine core and has to move into her masculine which is not her natural essence to make up for your perceived weakness. That makes her fearful and bitchy.

Women want to be in their feminine energy. Feminine energy is about opening up to receive love, bonding, connection, etc. You didn't penetrate her with your love and presence. That is usually when guys say: *Well, she says one thing, and then when I do what she says she wants, it makes her mad. She told me everything was fine and to go out and play poker with my buddies when she was in the hospital. So I went out and played and now she's mad at me.*

Women want you to know instinctively what to do. They don't want to **teach** you how to be a man. They want you to already **know** how to do all these things. One area where women could do a better job is in helping their men understand. Most women just assume: *He'll figure it out.* Or: *He should already know these things. Why should I have to teach him?* But most men really **don't** know these things.

So when she says: *Oh, nothing's wrong,* and you **know** something is wrong, then you need to shut off the television and say: *Honey, what's the matter?* She: *Oh, I'm fine. I don't want to talk about it right now.* **NOT.** That is a test. It is her saying: *How much do you really care about me? Are you willing to get past all these barriers and these blocks I'm putting in your way to find out what is going on or not?*

She: *I don't want to talk about it.* Me: *I'm not going anywhere.* Then I'll start using some humor. I will sit there, if she's in the kitchen or something and say: *What's wrong?* She: *I'm not talking to you.* Me: *Okay, well, I'll just sit in here then,* and I'll start singing or something along the lines of: *Jimmy crack corn and I don't care...* I'll start throwing little things like almonds at her. If she's putting dishes away, I'll start taking dishes out and put them back on the counter. I'll just be really silly and goofy.

Then she'll say: *What do you want? Why are you bothering me?* I'll say: *I'm not bothering you. I just want to know what's on your mind.* She: *I'm not talking about it.* Me: *Okay, you're not talking about it. So tell me what's **really** on your mind.* She: *I'm not talking about it.* Me: *Well, what's eating at you then?*

She: *I'm not speaking to you. You pissed me off.* Me: *Oh? I pissed you off, huh? So what are you mad about? Talk to me. I want to know, honey. Tell me. Communicate. I want to know what's on your mind.* Now I have finally broken through and started on hitting the root of the problem. She: *I really, **really** don't want to talk about it right now.* Me: *Well, I'm not going anywhere.* Then I'll go over and shut the water off, and close the dishwasher. I'll hold her. She may squirm and push me away and say: *Don't touch me.* Then I might start tickling her or pinch her nipples playfully. When they get hard I will say, *is it cold in here?* or *Are you cold or something?* She'll say *you're a jerk!* I'll say *I like when your nipples are hard. It turns me on! Have I ever told you how sexy you look with hard nipples?*

I'll pull up her shirt and blow on her belly or something, being silly and outrageous, just to get her out of that state. It's called a pattern interrupt. She is now seeing that no matter what she does, she can't sway me from my purpose. My purpose is to find out what's wrong, what's on her mind. My purpose is to give her the love that she is really looking for. My life is a drama free zone and I'm simply not going to put up with drama. I am only having fun and being playful.

I'm the man and I set the tone… always. If I were to give into her attempt at drama and negativity, I'm letting her be the leader. That would only make things worse. Women don't want the power anyway. Be her rock. Her mountain.

Eventually she may just break down, start crying and tell me just what's going on. I will keep working to pull it out of her: *What's the matter? How did it make you feel?* When she tells me: *Well, you did this, this, and this, and it really bothered me.* I will repeat some of that back to her and say: *So when I did this, and I said that, it really hurt your feelings, and made you upset.*

When you communicate with women, you have to find out what's going on: *Honey, what's bothering you?* If she says: *Oh, I'm fine*, and you **know** something's wrong, then you can't walk away. If you walk away, she may throw a dish at you as if to say: *I can't believe you.* Me: *What? You told me nothing's wrong.* That's an extreme example, and no, women don't throw things at me, nor would I tolerate that kind of hostility, but you get my point. Google "Corey Wayne When She Pisses You Off" on how to properly set boundaries with women.

You have to dig deeper, because she is testing to see if you **really** care enough to want to know what's bothering her. If you **really** care enough to take away the pain she's feeling inside, you need to draw this out of her by asking her questions: *Honey, tell me what's upsetting you*, and not leaving until you get it out of her what is going on.

Most guys will just say: *I'm sorry*, and she'll say: *Okay, thank you. I'm glad you're sorry.* Or the guy says: *I love you.* Instead of you **saying** it, she wants you to **show** it. The way you show it is with your presence, and by showing her: *You are not moving me off center, here.* The words don't really have that much meaning to her. It is your actions, and the fact that you are not going anywhere. It is you **understanding** her when she says: *Well, you did this, this, this, and it really hurt me*, and you repeat it back: *Oh, so I did this, this, and this, and it made you feel this way. And it hurt you, and it made you feel like this. Is that right? Is that how I made you feel?*

Keep working to pull it out of her: *Tell me everything. Don't leave anything out*, and after she pauses: *Tell me more*, and: *How'd that make you feel?* Every few minutes or so when she shares something with you, in order to create rapport with her, you are going to repeat back to her some of the things she just said to you.

So you are telling me that the other day when I left without kissing you goodbye in the morning, it made you feel like I didn't care about you. It was as though I didn't appreciate that you woke up extra early to get the kids ready and to make me breakfast. Am I hearing you correctly? Is that what you meant?

So basically, I hurt your feelings the other day. You need to acknowledge this. *I'm sorry, honey. I was just in a hurry, rushing out the door like that, not taking the time to thank you for breakfast, and getting the kids ready. It was wrong of me not to appreciate you. It was wrong of me not to acknowledge that. It was wrong of me not to give you that. I know that was all you were looking for, was that little peck on the cheek, or that little kiss, but you're right. I was really focused on what I was going to be doing during the day, and I know I was being selfish. I was only thinking about myself, and not thinking about you. I took you for granted, totally, and I'm sorry.*

That is the way you need to apologize to a woman. Most guys will say: *Well, I **said** I was sorry for not kissing you goodbye.* You didn't take the time to find out **exactly** what was going on. You didn't take the time to repeat some of it back to her and create rapport. You didn't take the time to put it into the context of how it hurt her emotionally by breaking through her barriers. Remember: *Women have an emotionally based operating system.* You need to keep working with her, pulling the information out, until you hear those magic words: *I feel so much better, I'm so glad we talked.*

Usually, that is what you'll get. Until you get that, you are not done. You haven't completely opened her back up. And if it's things that have been building up for a long time, you may be a couple hours. Each time, you will get a little better at it. You'll be able to get it down to 15-20 minutes. Then, when something really sets her off, it will only take you 15-20 minutes to get her to that point where she is saying: *I feel so much better. I'm so glad we talked.*

Those are the magic words, but not necessarily in that order. She might say: *I feel better.* Or: *Oh, I'm good now, honey. I'm glad we talked. I'm glad I got this off my chest.* When you hear that, you know you have gotten through and the barriers are down. Then you can hold her in your arms, and you can love her. You can make love *to* her – because she's open again to you at that point.

Women want to be understood. Now you know how to understand your lady by talking about her feelings and getting everything off her chest that has been bothering her deep inside. When you finally get to the root cause of everything that's bothering her, you will hear those magic words: *I feel better. I'm so glad we talked.*

Keep in mind that with a woman, you get no points for what you did in the past. You could have been the perfect husband for the past ten years, but if you've been screwing up all day today, she will say: *You are a jerk, a bad husband, and you never treat me right.* Most guys will respond: *Well, I did this last week and this the week before. I've been married to you for ten years and I have always done this and...* Guys go on this whole rationalizing thing.

Women don't think like that. All she is trying to say to you is: *You hurt me in this moment and you need to make it right.* You do not get points for what you did in the past. What you did for the first ten years of the marriage doesn't matter. What **does** matter to her is that you've been screwing up today. She doesn't **literally** mean you are a bad husband or a jerk. This is what she is feeling **right now**, in the moment she is saying it. She is riding the wave of emotion. It is just the place that women come from.

When she brings up things from the past you thought were resolved, she's simply communicating that you have hurt her in the same way you did previously in the past. Don't take it personally. Women use relational examples to communicate their feelings. It's implicit communication not explicit communication.

Women are emotionally based. I always hear guys saying: *Women aren't rational.* I say: *To me they are completely rational, once you understand where they are coming from.* When you understand that everything they say and do is emotionally based.

The Art of Knowing

The art of knowing the right and wrong things to do with and around a woman can be a tricky path to walk. It is a lot easier when you use some common sense. For example: *Don't talk about other women.* Come on guys, how bright do you have to be to figure **that** one out?

If you are at the beach, don't say: *Hey, that's a really nice bikini that girl's wearing.* Or: *She's got some really nice sunglasses.* Your woman knows you are comparing her to that woman. **Do not** tell her how you really liked it when your ex-girlfriend used to do this and used to do that. Or how your new boss wears her hair long and straight and really nice, and that she was wearing this really nice, tight dress…

A woman knows that when you comment on another woman, you are making a comparison. They certainly don't like it. Why would you go out of your way to make her miserable?

Now if she is noticing another man, she may be bringing it up just to test you. It may be her way of saying: *Will you pay more attention to me now?* It also could be an indication that maybe things aren't going as well as you think they are in your relationship, so she's noticing another guy. It is her way of saying: *Hey buddy, you'd better get your act together, because my attraction is dropping.* It is important to be aware of that.

You never want to argue with a woman, because it is only going to escalate. The bottom line is that you are never going to win an argument anyway. Women don't fight fair, and they don't argue rationally. Their arguments are mostly emotionally based. If you are trying to have a rational argument with her, she will only end up throwing around more of her emotions, because she is trying to say: *Hey, you need to notice me. You need to acknowledge my heart. You need to acknowledge how I feel.* You are not doing that by arguing. When I talk to clients who are arguing with their women I know they do not understand women. It is impossible for guys who don't understand women to have effortless and drama-free relationships.

All arguing will do is to cause her to argue more, raise her voice, throw more emotions into the mix, and possibly to cry, scream, and do all the other things she may do. It is more productive to take a metal hammer and beat yourself over the head than it is to try to argue with a woman.

If you have just screwed up and she brings up something that happened ten years ago, it is just her way of trying to drive the point home. She is bringing up other times you wounded her in the same way. You can't take it personally. She is trying to say: *Hey, listen to me. I want you to understand me.* The communication technique I covered previously is what you need to use to get through and acknowledge her.

One of the other things to keep in mind, as it invariably comes up at some point with your girlfriend or your wife, where she will see a very attractive woman and say: *Do you think that woman over there is pretty?* Most guys will look over and say: *Oh, yeah.* What I will often do to show her I really adore her is to respond with: *Where?* Or… *Yea, she's hot, but not as hot as you, baby.*

Girlfriends of mine have done this while I'm sitting at dinner. She will say: *Look at the girl over there.* I'll continue to look my girlfriend in the eyes and say: *I don't see her.* She: *The one right over there.* I'll say: *I don't know what you're talking about.* Even though I'm sure there is a very pretty woman over there, it is my way of saying: *I could care less about the woman on the other side of the restaurant. You are the only one I care about.* I also might playfully say, *What? You want to have a threesome with her?*

I might even say something like: *You are the most beautiful woman in the world, and the only one that matters to me.* It is a subtle way of showing her that she has all of my presence. In her own subtle way, she is looking to see how you react to another woman. I take that as an opportunity to show her how into *her* I am, and how committed I am.

Weathering the Storm

Women are like the ocean, and guys have these little rowboats or canoes. A guy will be just cruising along and it's a nice, sunny, beautiful day, and he's thinking: *Wow. This is great.*

The ocean is flat, then all the sudden, from out of nowhere it becomes like a hurricane. There are ten-foot waves everywhere. The guy, no matter *what* his lady is doing, has to remain centered. In other words, he can't let her capsize his boat. He can't let her sink him. He can't let her get him off his path and his purpose in life. And he can't – no matter what – let her get him out of his masculine.

If she does capsize your boat and you sink? First, you have to bail it out and bring it back to the surface. Now she will make it twice as hard, the storm will get twice as bad, until she sees that no matter what she does, she can't sway you from your path. It doesn't matter if she's yelling, cussing at you, or saying: *I hate your guts.*

The movie, Cinderella Man, is a great example of how a woman tests the purpose of her man, and tests his strength and masculinity. Based on a true story, Jim Braddock, the boxer, had been out of boxing for two years due to an injury. A promoter friend comes to him and says: *Hey, I've got a fight. It's a one-time shot. I need you to fight tomorrow night.* He had one day's notice without training and ends up beating the guy. So with zero training and no fights for two years, he takes a fight, beating a potential championship contender. He was never expected to win. They had basically needed a warm body in the ring.

In a nutshell, he goes all the way to the heavyweight championship bout, and the guy he is fighting for the heavyweight championship has previously killed two guys. He's really young, and an amazing fighter. His wife tells him not to fight because he'll get hurt, or worse, he will die.

However, masculine energy demands that he fight and go live his purpose, no matter how much his wife protests. If he were to quit, or to not fight, or shrink in the face of the challenge, then he would be weak. He is a hero that everyone can believe in. Even when his wife protests, and tests, he still fights, even if it means losing everything. Even if it means that she is not going to support him. This is masculine energy.

His wife, at one point in the movie, goes into the church to pray for him before the fight. The church is full. She goes to the priest: *What's everybody in here for? I'm coming to pray for Jimmy.* He tells her: *Everyone in here is praying for him. They're praying that he's going to win and that he's going to be okay.*

At the time, during the Depression, he was a guy that had been down and out, and completely out of boxing, but he managed to get a second chance at his dream. Now he is fighting for the championship. Even though he shouldn't have won all these fights, he was winning because he had a reason to win. He was doing it to provide for his family. They needed the money, and he did not want his family to get split up.

He almost lost his whole family. At one point he and his wife sent their kids away to live with relatives because they didn't have the money to feed them properly. Their power had been turned off, it was cold, the kids were getting sick, and his circumstances created so much pain inside of him that he was not going to let this happen.

So he was out there fighting a boxing match and he was fighting for his family, for their survival and well-being. His wife, needless to say, was stunned that everybody in the church was praying for him. Everybody in that church wanted a hero to believe in, especially during the Great Depression. They wanted someone to give them hope that things would turn out for the best, even when they looked at their worst. You can imagine what the Great Depression was like.

The people thought he was fighting for them. This made them feel safe. He gave them hope and certainty, which is exactly what masculine energy does when it is in its core. It also has the same effect on a woman's feminine heart. Her feminine heart opens to receive his presence when he passes her test, and tests of his manhood.

At one point in the movie his wife told him: *I'm not coming to the fight. I don't want you to fight. I'm not happy that you're fighting. I'm not going to listen to it on the radio. I'm not supporting you in this, at all.*

Regardless, he told her: *This is what I do. I'm a fighter. I'm fighting for you, and I'm fighting for the kids. I'm going to do this.* In essence, he was telling her: *I don't care how much you protest. I have to do this. This is my purpose.*

His wife bluffed saying: *I don't support this at all.* He leaves, calling her bluff. Right before the fight, she shows up at the locker room and gives him a hug and kiss, basically letting him know that she is submissive at that point. She goes along with what he's saying, and supports him. He called her bluff and she backed down, accepting that he was in his masculine. I think it is a really great example of masculine and feminine energy, because again, feminine energy will sometimes bluff to test.

His wife had come to him before the fight, and says she would not support it. In other words, she threatened to walk, or not support him if he fights. He, again, remains indifferent. He goes anyway, because he has to. Because that's his purpose, that's his mission, because that's what he must do, as a strong, masculine man.

He is a superior man who will give everything for his purpose. That included his life. That is why men go off to war, and will die willingly. It's because that is just what masculine energy does. You must be this way for your lady, or she will never trust your core.

He is the first of the boxers to walk into the arena. It is completely silent, which is something that has never happened before. Everybody in the crowd really wants him to win, because he is such an underdog. Someone shouts out in the crowd: *You can do it, Jimmy!* Then the whole crowd cheers and goes nuts.

This is what happens to your lady when you don't shrink in the face of her storm. No matter what she throws at you, she can't rock your boat. She can't dump you in the water. She can't knock you over. You have to be her rock.

In the end, Jim wins the fight and he owns his lady's heart. He told her it would be okay and it was. At the end of the movie, they rolled the credits. In WWII, he was called to duty, and went to serve his country. He served honorably. I'm sure that not only his wife, but any other woman will tell her man: *Stay here where it is safe. I don't want anything to happen to you.*

But again, masculine energy when it is in its core has to go. Even though she would have rather he hadn't gone off to war, she loved him more because he did. He was willing to sacrifice his life and everything for his family, and for his country. That makes the feminine woman feel safe. He is willing to sacrifice everything to protect her, to make sure that she's okay. He takes all her pain and worry upon himself, so she doesn't have to experience those emotions.

Women Don't Lie – Men Don't Listen

She may have told you that she was totally head over heels in love with you, and five minutes later say she hates your guts. When she says she hates your guts – that is what she is feeling right then and there in that moment. Five minutes ago when she told you she loved you, she *did* love you five minutes ago. But what she's feeling right now, in this moment, is: *I hate your guts.*

Again, it doesn't matter if you did everything perfect for the first ten years you were together. What matters is that you screwed up five minutes ago, and now there's hell to pay. Now you have to weather the storm, break through her barriers, and get back to her heart. You need to get her back in her feminine energy so she can open back up and be that playful, beautiful woman you love. You do this by using humor and understanding, and by letting her know that you are not going anywhere until you get to the bottom of it.

A man usually doesn't understand it when his woman walks out on him. She has been telling him all along: *You are never around. You never spend any time with me. We never talk. You don't care about what I want.* These are the things that a woman does to get your attention, and that most guys just completely ignore. They don't take her seriously, invalidating the way she is feeling at the moment. If you are invalidating her emotions, and she is an emotionally based creature, how long do you think she is going to take it?

The Secret Language of Women

Women have their own secret language, and yet they expect men to understand it. ***Pay attention guys***. It is not what she ***says***, but what she ***does*** that is the key to breaking this code. They are more subtle in their responses, instead of direct, like men. For example: You ask a woman something and she responds with: *I'll think about it.*

It means no. Chances are, she may have put on a bland face to go with that remark, but if you are watching closely, you can catch the clues in her face.

If you ask a woman you just met for her phone number and she says: *Well, I don't give it out, but why don't you give me one of your business cards?* It means: *I'm not interested.* As I mentioned before, we have trained women not to reject us to our face, so they have had to develop more subtle ways of getting around to saying: *No.*

It is about understanding what all the cues mean. When a woman says: *You never listen to me.* Or: *You never do this for me or that for me.* In that moment, it is what she's feeling. It doesn't mean that you have never, ever done this or that for her. All it means is in ***that*** moment, you are failing as a man to give her the presence that she is looking for from you.

That is why women tend to generalize a lot when they are saying things. They will say: *I can't stand you*, or: *You're such a jerk*, or she gets really mad and says she hates you. It doesn't mean that she does not love you any more, but right then and there, in that moment, she is feeling that she hates your guts because you failed.

She may be completely shut down to you. By your presence and communicating with her, you are going to work to open her back up. Once she is back open, she will usually apologize for what she said, with something like: *I was just really emotional.* Or she may be all over you and say: *I love you!* That is just her being a woman. It is part of the weathering of the storm.

Understanding the secret language is about understanding what her responses mean. Guys think logically and women think emotionally. Most of the time, women giving advice on other women are not going to come out and say: *Well, she doesn't like you.* They do not want to come right out and tell you the things that hurt your feelings.

The more pauses a woman uses during speaking is an indication that she is thinking hard about how to try and word something. Listen carefully to her wording at this point. She is trying very hard not to be impolite or rude, but the actual words and where she places inflections on those words will tell you exactly what she is trying to say.

For example, you go up to a woman and say: *Is anyone sitting here?* Compare these statements: *No, it's open.* Or she hesitates, shrugs, looks down or away and says: *...No...It's open.* The first one says that the seat is open and you are welcome to sit next to her. The second one says: *If you really have to. The seat is open, but I'd rather you left it that way.*

With a guy, language is like simplistic, straightforward dog commands: *Sit, stay, lie down, and roll over*. With a woman, it is like the cat analogy. You have to read her actions. You always judge a woman by what she does, and not what she says. If she breaks a date and then tells you that she can't wait to see you again in the same sentence – the bottom line is that she still broke the date. That tells me that she has a very low attraction and she doesn't really care to see me. When she says: *But I can't wait to see you again,* it is her way of trying to make you feel good, and not be upset or mad at her for breaking the date.

She hopes you will just figure it out. Women will understand what that response means. Most guys don't understand what that response means.

Part IX:

Taking it to the Next Level

Sharing of Yourself

In past chapters, I have talked about sharing as little information about yourself as possible, to be a mystery to a woman, to build the anticipation. Instead of telling her about you, you force her to ask about you. There will come a time, when you move closer into the steps of a committed relationship, that you will be asked to share more of who you are with your lady. It is **not** okay, however, to unload all of your negative baggage into your lady's lap for her to deal with.

At some point in a long-term relationship, it is inevitable that things are going to come up and you are going to share the challenges you have had in your life. If you are going to share all your baggage, you want to put a positive spin on it, such as how it helped you grow, and how you are a better person because of it. You don't want to talk negatively about things. To give an example:

Being divorced, I can tell my story in two different ways:

I was married when I was in my mid-20s. I married a woman I shouldn't have married. It was **not** a good marriage. We were **always** fighting, and we didn't get along. She was **always** pissing me off. She **never** seemed to make any sense. It was **extremely** difficult.

I ended up leaving after a year, because I just couldn't take it any more. We even had a dog together. I moved out. She changed the locks on me and I couldn't get my bills. It was a real pain in my butt, and I had to call her father to have him help me get my bills.

Then she started dating another guy, and he was living in *my* house. I was paying for *all* the utilities and *all* the bills. After the marriage ended, when we finally got the divorce, I didn't date anybody for six months. The whole thing had been really tough. It beat me up emotionally. It took me several years to get over it. I just did not want to be in a relationship for many years.

That is a very negative way to tell the story. The way I have always told it is:

Yes. I was married in my mid-20s. I married somebody I shouldn't have married. I didn't love her in the way that she deserved to be loved, and vice versa. We were not what each other really wanted. The relationship was great. It was a gift because it helped me grow. Eventually I found the strength to stand up for what I really wanted. It also helped to give her the freedom to find somebody that was going to give her *all* their attention, *all* their presence, and *all* their love, which is what she really deserved. It left me free to go out and find somebody that I could really be happy with.

You can put a negative spin on things, or you can put a positive spin on it. If you put a negative spin on it, and you keep talking about negative things, you will lower her attraction. Nobody wants to be around someone that is negative all the time.

One thing that is really big in our culture today is that on all the talk shows and movies, the guy is supposed to talk about his feelings, get all his baggage out on the table, and talk about all this crap. At the end of the day, if you are always telling your wife or your girlfriend something that is negative, and you are constantly putting a negative spin on it, it's making her associate negative feelings with you. It is not going to make her love you more.

She will appreciate you for being honest, but the effect that it has on her attraction is that it will drop. You will look weak in her eyes. She will sense weakness, she will pull away, and she will test you more. I think it *is* good to share things, but before you do, think first: *If I tell her this, is it going to have a positive effect on her attraction toward me, or is it going to have a negative effect?*

If there is a very negative event that you feel the need to share with her, put a positive spin on it. Let her know that it's not deflating you, or destroying you. Face it. If you are coming home every single day and talking about all the problems and all the things that are going wrong in your life, you are going to lower your wife's or your girlfriend's attraction to you.

Love is fun. It is something you are supposed to enjoy. So again, think it over: *Does she really need to know this information? Is it going to help the relationship? Is it going to make her love you more?* Nine times out of ten, if it's something negative, the answer is going to be: *No*.

Yes. I do agree you need to share things, but you have to put a positive spin on it. Come from a place of: *This is something that really helped me grow*, or: *This challenge we are facing right now – I know I'm going to be a better person because of it*. If you really want to wallow in your sorrow and feel sorry for yourself, those are the things you need to do with your guy friends.

Your guy friends are the ones that will take it for a little while, but eventually they are going to tell you: *Man, you've got to cut this crap out. You're bringing **me** down.* Nobody likes somebody that is always a downer.

The Gift

You do not buy a woman gifts. Why? They come off as a bribe for sex. You really don't buy a woman anything until she is completely head over heels in love with you. Don't send flowers as an apology. Send them as a surprise to your girlfriend. I used to do this a lot. I used to send flowers after the first date. Women respond by saying: *Oh, this is so nice...* but it's really not helping. You are giving away all the mystery. You are letting her know: *I really like you. I like you so much that I'm sending you flowers.* It's too much too soon and communicates a lack of understanding of how attraction works. Plus it comes off as a bribe for sex.

It doesn't leave her wondering. The goal is that you want her to wonder. She enjoys discovering her feelings. She enjoys letting those feelings grow. Women are just dying to chase the guy.

Too many guys will start buying expensive jewelry and flowers, and all kinds of things. In the first two months, especially, those kinds of things need to be off limits. Those are the types of things you save for special occasions, and only after she's in love with you.

If she is a giver, you have passed the first couple months of the relationship, and she is totally in love with you, she will start buying you little things here and there. One thing you can look at is that more than likely, in the first two months, a woman is not buying you any gifts. After you have been together for several months, she's in love with you, and it's her birthday... then you can buy her something nice – but don't over do it.

Guys with money will usually start buying gifts right away. I mentioned that one friend of mine earlier in the book. She has four or five different engagement rings she has collected over a few short years. Seriously, she will meet a guy and start dating him, and on the first, second or third date, he will say: *I'm going to marry you*, and proceed to start buying her jewelry, and necklaces. She hardly knows this guy and he is spending thousands and thousands of dollars on gifts and trinkets for her. Buying expensive gifts only shows that you are needy and trying to bribe her.

You are teaching her early on to expect these things all of the time. Wait at least for the first several months to pass. Until she is completely in love with you, don't buy her anything. It is ***not*** going to make her want you more.

Do not pay her bills, rent, or any of these things unless you are actually living together, or you are married. One of the guys I have been coaching is a great guy, and very successful. He is also a very nice and caring person. He bought this woman he has been seeing an engagement ring. It came to the point where he was paying her rent, giving her money, and even gave her a job working for one of his companies.

She had not reached the point where her attraction level was a 9. She was not head over heels in love with him, and he was doing way too much for her, far too soon in the relationship. She has taken advantage of his weakness, and now he has come to me to get the situation turned back around. I have met so many men over the years that, even though they are only going out with a woman once in a while, they are paying her rent, giving her money, and doing all of these things for her. I had a close family member buy a woman he was no longer sleeping with a condo because she was broke. He gave her money, paid her bills, bought her supplements, etc. She put him in the friend zone and he deluded himself into believing he could bribe her with money. Unless a woman is head over heels in love with you and you are living with her, you should not be doing these kinds of things. You are showing weakness. She will take advantage of it until she finds someone else who can be the strong, centered man that she truly needs and wants.

It Feels Like Making Love

As with the rest of the relationship, you want to move slowly into the lovemaking, building the anticipation for it. Also, just like the rest of the relationship, the woman will let you know when she is ready to move toward this step. Obviously, lovemaking is a step that can have bigger ramifications on the dating relationship.

With affection and making love, you want to continue building the anticipation. Maybe first going out for dinner, and then you find yourself alone with her at your place, or maybe you are back at her place. The first stage is just gentle caressing. You are going to kiss her for a few minutes, and then stop and back off. Talk for a little while, and then grab her and start kissing her again.

Each time, you go a little bit further. Start kissing her, and show her a little affectionate caressing. Run your hands through her hair. Touch the back of her neck – that is one of the most sensual places on a woman, actually. Run your fingers gently up and down her neck, or across her face. Show her a lot of affection and kiss her – and then back off, stop, and talk for a little bit more. Take two steps forward, one step back.

She may come to you and start kissing you more. Keep building anticipation, and take your time. By stopping and leaning back, you cause her to want to move forward, and to anticipate it. Eventually, you will have her so wound up that she just can't take it any more. It is the whole process. It is the undressing of her clothes. It is just one little thing at a time. You are massaging her and caressing her. You are running your fingers up and down her arm, touching her hair…

Most guys go right for the sexual parts. This is sheer anti-anticipation. If you have done a great job the whole evening, the more you wind her up, the better the experience is going to be for her. It is ultimately going to be better for you, too. You are going to feel more successful. It is easy for a guy to get satisfied by having sex, but for the woman, it is the whole process – the backing off a little bit, moving forward a little bit. It's like you take two steps forward, one step back. Two steps forward and then one step back. It is a constant building of anticipation. When you encounter resistance, don't stop or give up. Just lean back and chat for a few minutes, then take another run at her a few minutes later. Each time you will get further and further until you've taken all her clothes off. If you still have some clothes on, you'll have to take those off and strap on a love glove. Sex must be the man's fault. You penetrate her after all. It's about slowly breaking down her resistance until she feels safe and comfortable enough to let you have your way with her.

At the same time, the sensual caressing intermingled with the kissing and the talking, opens her up emotionally. Women have to have their emotions engaged before they feel safe having sex.

By building the anticipation in the way I have described, you are actually helping to engage their emotions into the act itself. That is when the experience becomes so much more intense for a woman, and so much more pleasurable. The building anticipation engages their emotions and actually tends to heighten a woman's sensitivity to the intimacy of the sexual act.

Again, women are emotion-based, and men are purpose-driven. When he can really pleasure his lady, a guy feels successful. The more pleasure she has, the more successful he feels.

I have always used this technique in my own relationships, and I've been amazed by the effect it has. I love it when you are giving your woman oral sex, and she just can't take it any more. She tells you that she wants you inside of her. It's driving her nuts.

Most of the time, you want to take your time with that. If she says she wants you to penetrate her right now, wait a few minutes. Let the anticipation build a little bit more. It's also like when you are having sex with a woman, and she says: *I want you to cum now.* Don't do that on command either; you want to hold off a few minutes.

It is another subtle way of her feeling your strength, and it builds even more anticipation. That was a big one for me. Once I learned that, I was amazed at the results. With one woman I dated, there would always be this point when we were having sex and she'd say: *I want you to cum now.* When I first started dating her, I would, and we would have our orgasm at the same time.

One time I decided I was just not going to obey her commands. She was on top of me and we just kept going. She had a really good orgasm, and said: *You haven't cum yet.* We just kept having sex, and she was able to have one after another, just bam, bam, bam, bam, eight orgasms. It was amazing. I felt so good about that.

I loved that I was able to give her so much pleasure. The key was in building the anticipation and how I kept building it more and more. She tried taking control of the finish, and I would give it to her eventually, but on my terms. It would be when I was ready to do it. It drove her wild, as it has every woman I've ever been with. That has been my experience. She wants to feel your strength. Your ability to resist her even though you want her.

It also goes back to the woman not being able to have her way with you. It makes her feel safe. It makes her completely open up to you. They know that you can completely have your way with her and still protect her, protect her heart, and make her feel safe.

One of the other things I would like to point out is that sometimes, say when the man's doing the oral sex thing, and she is saying: *I want you inside of me right now*. Or if you are having sex and she does that on-command thing where it's: *I want you to come right now*. It may not always be because she is trying to test you or take control of the sexual act.

There are situations where the man is just not pleasing her in the right way. That is another one of those "secret language of women" things. She is trying to move it toward a conclusion, maybe because you are not necessarily doing something right. It may be even uncomfortable, or sometimes a little painful. Or what you are doing could be working, but it's not working at the level she needs it to be at to become fully engaged. Google "Corey Wayne How Men Can Have Multiple Orgasisms."

Rather than assuming that everything is being done right and just holding back, one of the things you may want to try is to do something different than what you were already doing. Try a different stroke, or shift position a little bit. See if she pulls you back to what you were doing, or see if she is better enjoying the new thing. Sometimes a woman is directing you to get it over with, because you are not satisfying her the way she wants to be satisfied. Say to her: *tell me what you like. Tell me where and how you want to be touched and how much pressure to apply* as your giving her oral sex or having sex. You must ask good quality questions. Most people do not.

Every woman is different. Some like it one way, and some like it another way. Some go bananas with oral sex, some go bananas when they're on top, and some go bananas with doggie style. They are all different. With some of them, their nipples are extremely sensitive and it drives them berserk to touch them, and some it doesn't do much for at all.

Using the same technique with each woman is neither good nor bad. Again, you should be watching for her response. Because if you are doing something that she does not like, you will see her become distracted. You will see that she is either trying to direct you into a different direction, or she's just trying to get it over with, or she may become distracted. Pay attention.

The Final Commitment

So how do you know when it is time to propose? Once again, the woman will let you know. Basically, women are going to say things along the lines of: *When are we getting married? Are we ever going to get married? Where is this going?* This is obviously after they are in love. This is their way of saying: *I'm ready.*

Now, the question: *Where is this going?* That could also apply to the transitional phase we were talking about before, and not just to marriage. It could mean: *Are we just going to keep on dating, or are we going to move into a more committed type relationship?* But if you have been paying attention to all her signs of attraction, you should know very well what your woman is asking you.

If there is any doubt, or even if you just want to be playful, you could always respond to that question with: *Well, what do you mean?* Then her real meaning or intent behind that will come out. She will let you know. Women usually get to a certain point where they say: *Unless we get married...* Basically, they just come out and give a guy an ultimatum, eventually.

I have a story that illustrates the importance of watching all the signs a woman is giving you. It demonstrates the necessity of always paying attention to her attraction level. Too many men project their own attraction level onto a woman and just assume she is as interested in him as he is in her.

I was on a European cruise back in 2001. I was doing a lot of advertising on one of the local television stations and I was there with my business partner. There was also another guy on the cruise, a very well known doctor.

He was on the cruise with his wife. She was a former model, and drop dead gorgeous. I always love talking to women. This was back when I was really starting to get things, so we were sitting there talking. I have this way with women, where I can just pull this stuff out of them. She just opened right up.

She told me about how they met, and that they dated for a couple years. She also proceeded to tell me that when she married him, she wasn't even in love with him. It got me thinking. He was completely successful, and observation told me he was not a completely centered guy. She had been married to him for two years before she actually, finally fell in love with him.

That is why it is so important to pay attention to all the signs of a woman's attraction level in you. There are women out there that will date and marry guys when they are not in love with them. It doesn't matter whether it is low self-esteem, or they are looking for security. You want to marry somebody that is head over heels in love with you. This guy happened to luck out.

Just imagine. All the time he was dating her he had no idea. He married her, she went along with it, and he had no idea. He may still not even know that it wasn't until two years after they were married that she actually fell in love with him. What if she had never fallen in love with him? He would have never experienced the bliss of being in love.

It is a perfect example of a guy completely focused on his own attraction, and how he projected it onto his girlfriend, his fiancé, and his wife. That's why what I have been telling you all along is so important. Obviously she wasn't saying: *When are we going to get married?* He was completely driving the whole relationship, and she was just kind of going along with everything.

I didn't ask her that specific question, but I suspect she wasn't the one to initiate the thoughts of marriage. I could just tell as soon as I met her husband. I sized him up and could feel his energy. He is a very successful doctor, don't get me wrong. He just had no idea how to read her. She told me that she pretty much went along with everything he wanted to do, even when she wasn't in love with him.

I could remember thinking: *Why would you marry a guy if you weren't in love with him?* Luckily for him, she eventually did fall in love with him. You see some of these guys out there that have achieved a tremendous level of success, but they get married to someone who's basically with them for the security aspect of it. It is not what I would want to do. When you are with someone who is head over heels in love with you, they are a lot more fun to be with than with someone that's just kind of dating you.

Part X: Keeping It All Together

The Care and Feeding of Women

I want to go back to revisit the concept of how beautiful women bluff in order to test you. For example, the woman I met on the retreat who basically kept saying: *I don't like you. I'm going to leave. You're a jerk.* You can't allow yourself to be affected by a woman. That is one of the important points I want to make about the care and feeding of women. Google "Corey Wayne Indifference Makes The Difference With Women."

If a woman's attraction level is a 5 and you are doing everything right, she will not find herself able to walk away from you. She will be drawn back to you, and will probably not even understand why. That pure, feminine core will react to your strong, masculine center, and she will not be able to turn away from you. She is like a moth to a flame, although in this case, the flame is not danger, it is safety. She is drawn to you; instinctively **knowing** deep inside that you can make her feel safe. The only way she will be able to walk away and **stay** away is if her attraction level is below a 5. If she doesn't come back, her attraction level was never above 5 to begin with.

When I first started understanding all of these concepts, I was scared to **death** to try this one out. It was the exact opposite of everything I had come to believe about women. I tried it anyway, and was amazed at how well it worked. A woman is just unable to walk away from a strong, centered guy that is doing everything right to show her that he is in his masculine.

The concepts I have taught you from the beginning of this book need to be applied throughout your dating and relationship life. This includes having fun, listening to your lady and really hearing what she is saying, always judging her attraction, continuing to build the anticipation, remaining in your masculine, staying in your center, and never letting a woman push you off that center. A relationship is an on-going joy of giving of yourself, and giving to your lady. It also means knowing who you are and what you want out of life, and when to walk away if you are not getting what you need to be happy.

If you are doing everything right, and you *know* you are doing everything right, then some women are going to stick around, and some of them are going to walk away. Sometimes when they walk away it is only a bluff. Remember *Cinderella Man*, when his wife refused to support him, and she wasn't going to come to the fight, or even listen to it on the radio…?

She *did* come to the fight. She *did* wish him well. When she went back to the house, she *did* listen to the fight on the radio, even though she said she wasn't going to do it. It was her way of bluffing and testing his strength, and he did not let it affect him. It is important to keep in mind that if a woman walks, there is another bus coming by in fifteen minutes. Don't get hung up on one single woman when you are in the dating world.

Guys have to understand that women are going to do what they want, when they want, and with who they want. The bottom line is – well, that *IS* the bottom line. If you can grasp this concept, then all you need to do is to be a 3% man, and gently urge the woman or women you are interested in into the heights of anticipation that make *you* what it is they want, and who they want to do it with. You do this by following all of the things I have laid out in these pages.

Remember, human beings only retain about 10% of what we read or hear for the first time, so you will want to read this book at least ten times. All the books I have learned the most from are the ones I have read 10-15-20 times. When you *own* this material and you can live it, it *becomes* you. You own it. You just instinctively know, right away, where your lady's level of attraction is.

When a woman asks you: *Do you think I look fat in these jeans?* That is a loaded question. If she does look fat in the jeans, and you tell her: *No*, she's going to say: *You are not being honest.* If you tell her: *Yes, you do look fat in the jeans*, she's going to say: *You're mean. How could you say that?*

If your girlfriend or wife needs to lose weight, or if you feel she needs to exercise more, remember again that the feminine heart grows through praise. Avoid answering a question where there *is* no right answer or the *only* answers to that question are wrong answers. I will come back with something along the lines of: *Honey, those jeans aren't really important to me. I will tell you what I think is sexy: When I see you all sweaty in your workout outfit coming home from the gym. I just want peel off those sweaty clothes and have my way with you.*

That is praising her by saying: *I really like it when you work out. I think it's sexy when you are in your workout clothes and are working out.* As opposed to saying: *Boy, your ass is really fat.* Through praise, you are telling her what it is that you like, and what it is that you want.

If she sees you as 9 in the attraction level category, she wants to make you happy. So she is going to exercise, and she's going to go on a diet. She is going to lose the weight and do these things because you praised her in the right way.

A former girlfriend of mine used to come over to my house and exercise. She had gained a little bit of extra weight and would say: *Do you think I need to lose weight?* I responded to that by saying: *You use my treadmill all the time. What I really want is to see you on my treadmill, running naked. I think that is really sexy.* **That** is how you need to respond to those types of loaded questions.

She giggled and laughed. The next time I saw her on the treadmill, I said: *Why do you have your clothes on?* She said: *Because I'm working out.* I replied: *I told you I want to see you on there naked. That would be really sexy.* She kind of chuckled and laughed. It was a playful way of saying: *Hey, I really like what you're doing. I really like the fact that you are taking care of yourself.*

Keeping the Magic Alive

The simple concept is that what you do to get your lady to fall in love with you is what you have to do to keep her. If you don't date your wife or your girlfriend, some other guy eventually will.

One of the things I use a lot is humor, especially if I have done something that has really pissed my girlfriend off. After I know I have apologized appropriately for it, a lot of times I'll bring humor into it. I'll tease her. I'll banter back and forth just to get her to loosen up and get back into her feminine. My goal is to loosen her up to where she can be playful again. It is really important to use humor and be playful, and to not take things seriously. After all, the couple that plays together stays together.

It is very important to do these things because they make life so easy. Now you know what to do with your wife. You have to basically treat her as you did when you were courting her. You have to start dating her again. Then she will fall back in love with you and everything else will fall into place.

You are always going to be reading your woman's attraction in you, even if you have been married for 40 to 50 years. It is about keeping the romance alive, and playing together. The couple that plays together stays together. This is so true. What you do to get her is what you are going to have to do to keep her. As you long as you stay in your center and do not become complacent, the testing will be minimal. If the testing starts, you know you are not doing something right, and you need to switch gears. Recognize it for what it is: *An opportunity for growth and change from stagnation and complacency.*

One acquaintance of mine has been married to her husband for several years. They were struggling for a while, and both of them had to take on second jobs. It created a rut in an otherwise good relationship, which started her husband's slip downward into the pitfall of complacency. In the meantime, she was out waiting tables, and had a handful of regulars where she received the playful bantering she was missing from her husband.

There was one really good-looking guy in particular that came up regularly to flirt and banter with her. One morning, she woke up after having a particularly erotic dream that involved this good-looking guy. She decided to use it to test her husband, and give him one of those subtle women warning signs that she wasn't happy. She told him about the erotic dream involving one of her good looking customers, going even further to describe it as a very intense, sexual dream. She wanted to see how he would react.

Instead of pulling the jealousy thing, or even getting mad about it, his response to her was: *Why don't you come here and show me what happened in your dream?* She tested him, and he remained in his center. It was a great way for him to handle the situation. Not only did he pass the test, but he managed to replace her fantasy, the incidental dream, with him now in the starring role of her fantasy brought to life.

Basically, the way her husband responded was: *Oh really?* It's as though she had gone to a male strip bar, became really turned on, came home, and he said: *Hey, if that's what turns you on, come and share it with me. I'm ready to receive it. I'm a superior man. I'm not going to get jealous of this guy you had in your dreams. I'm not going to get jealous of the guy you met in the market.*

Women sometimes try to make their men jealous to shake them out of their complacency. If the man responds in the way this woman's husband did, she not only has the result she was looking for, but he never wavered off his center and now she was fully back in her feminine and open to him. When men respond badly to this kind of testing, women see it as a sign of weakness and neediness, and will test even more.

I love it when I see other guys staring at my girlfriend. To me it is a compliment, because I know who she is with, and at the end of the night, I know she is coming home with me. We will go out to dinner, to seminars, or wherever, and the guys are all trying to flirt with my girlfriend. I'll sit back and watch this happening. She will even tell them: *That's my boyfriend over there*, and they just completely ignore it. They continue on with their bad act, hoping she's going to slide them her phone number or whatever. And I know she's going home with me.

What if she was to do something inappropriate, when she was supposed to be totally in love with me? Then that is not the type of person I want to be with long term, anyway. I had a girl that I dated once that when I pissed her off, she would start hitting on my friends.

I remember once when we had just finished an amazing weekend together, and I had done something that upset her. This is when I was still learning. She called one of my best friends that still worked for me at the time, and asked to meet him out for drinks. It was her way of trying to make me jealous. I could never be with a woman like that, because I would have to always sleep with one eye open. What would happen if I married someone like that? I'd be away at a seminar or business meeting, and would be wondering the whole time: *What is she doing at home while I'm not there?*

That is one of the things I have on my list. I don't want somebody who is devious or dishonest. That was a quality that she had in spades. She learned it from her parents, because her parents did the same thing. They were always keeping secrets and lying to one another about the most stupid, little things. She learned to be manipulative from them: *I'll get another guy to try and make him jealous.* That was a total turn-off.

Normally, though, like I've said before, that stuff shouldn't sway you. It doesn't get a superior man off center, or out of his masculinity, or rock his boat in the stormy ocean. It is a test: *Does this make you jealous?*

The man who's wife had the dream handled it in such a way that he didn't get jealous, but he let her know that *he* wanted to be that focus of her attention. To continually blow it off when your woman is saying something to you, to never show any concern for whatever it is she needs from you to cause her to test you in the first place, is a signal to a woman that you don't care, or you are too complacent. As I mentioned earlier, once you are in your relationship, your lady wants your attention all the time.

Polarity is the Key to Maintaining Desire

I also want to revisit the discussion on masculine and feminine energy. The energy interacts a little differently in the long-term relationship than it does in the dating relationship.

Most women have a fantasy about being dominated. A woman wants the man to take control and handle everything. She has nothing to worry about, because he takes away all of her pain and worry. She wants to submit to all his love and strength, when he is centered and in his core.

After he has had a long day and comes home stressed, his lady, with a heart that is completely open, comes over and pours herself all over him with her beautiful feminine energy. It actually melts his stress away. There is only one way she is going to get to that place. She can only do that when she feels that he has completely taken over everything and she can be *completely* in her feminine and know her man is going to handle everything.

She can be playful, loving, and an absolute joy to be around. *The guy is her rock, and she is his joy*. A woman needs to feel as though no matter what happens, the bills, the rent, the things going on in everyday life, it is all taken care of. When I talk about a man taking a woman's pain away, it is all in their communication. No matter what goes on, how horrible her day has been, or how bad she feels, her man needs to know how to talk to her. He needs to know how to pull it out of her, how to open her up, and how to make her feel like he understands her.

So, even if everything is hitting the fan at work, and the bills are behind, it doesn't move him off center. He is the rock. When he is the rock, she doesn't have to worry about anything. Even if things aren't going well, she knows he will somehow find a way to turn it around.

If he is confident, says he is going to get things turned around, tells her not to worry about it, and she knows he can do that, she feels comfortable in opening up and basking in her feminine energy. As I have said, there is nothing more beautiful to me than a woman that is completely in her feminine, completely open. It is so alluring and so sexy to be drawn in by a woman like that.

This is in complete opposition to the woman I mentioned before where being with her was so hard to get her to get into her feminine. Even though she was physically stunning and perfect, I was, as a man, not extremely attracted to her. It was too much work to get her to get into her feminine. She was too business-oriented and in her masculine. It was so much work dating her that I had to stop.

In some rarer cases, there are those women that need a man to be more in his, well, not in his masculine. Maybe she needs to have a man more in his feminine to counteract who she is. Maybe that's who *she* wants in life. There are some guys out there that would rather be in the submissive role. There are men that are more in their feminine, and there are men that are completely in their masculine. There are women that are very less in their feminine than they are in their masculine, so they are going to attract those kind of energies. But it's the *essence of the core* of the individual that needs to be paid attention to.

For example, my core essence is masculinity. If you are completely in your masculine, you have to have a woman that is completely in her feminine. But if you are a guy that is kind of halfway in your feminine, halfway in you masculine, then you're going to be attracted to a woman that meshes with those core energies.

The problem is that it's going to be difficult to maintain polarity. That was what happened with this girl I was just telling you about. I had to work to get the polarity. The polarity wasn't there. So even though she was beautiful and drop dead gorgeous, I was just not drawn to her, because she was so into her masculine and it was too weird for me. It sort of turned my stomach and made me uneasy. It turned me off totally to who she was.

For most women, their natural essence is feminine. For most men, their natural essence is masculine. When a very feminine woman meets a guy whose essence really is masculine, but he is in his feminine when he approaches women, inside, she's naturally going to go: *Ewww.*

He may look like Brad Pitt, but she's going to have the same experience I had with the woman I was talking about. Even though her looks are physically beautiful, it makes it impossible to date her at that point. When a guy is in his feminine, even though he may be physically attractive to a woman that is very in her feminine, she is just not going to engage her emotions and be drawn to that guy.

From my experience, when a guy is really feminine at his core, and the woman is really feminine at her core, the polarity dissipates. I have seen relationships where these people are together and the woman is in charge and wears the pants in the family. Unfortunately, in my personal experience, it has been where the guy is a masculine guy, like the father of the woman that is more in her masculine. Her father was a masculine guy. When he is out with his guy friends, he is a guys' guy. But when he is with his wife, he's not comfortable with his masculinity. Most likely, he had a very domineering mother.

They've been married for about 30 years, but the polarity is not there. I mean, you can see what happens. The two start to look more and more alike. When the polarity is not there, the woman will often cut her hair real short, and many times will stop wearing make up. She doesn't put her femininity out there because she's been shut down so much by the weakness of the man she has chosen to be with, that she no longer feels attractive. She doesn't even *try* to get his presence any more, because she's just basically given up and resigned herself to the way that things are going to be.

A woman that is completely in her feminine *feels* very feminine. If she feels loved and adored by her husband – she will tend to keep her hair long. She will most likely wear make up. She often dresses up. She does the things that a feminine woman does.

You can go to the mall and tell which couples have been together for a long time. You will see the two of them with those t-shirts on that say: *I'm with stupid*, each one pointing at the other. Both are wearing baggy clothes and t-shirts, and they look alike. There is no polarity left in their relationship. They may have sex occasionally for a release, but they just don't treat each other the same as they did when they first started going out.

Here is another example. I have a friend of mine, who is a very masculine guy, but is a total wimp when he's around his wife. They have two kids together. When they first met, she was in very good shape, long red hair, and she wore make up. He was very weak, and let her run the household.

She finally cut off all of her hair, stopped wearing make up, stopped taking care of herself, and became very bitchy and very resentful. The last I heard, they have been married for like 10 to 12 years, and they haven't had sex in four years. They are staying in it for the kids.

This book is primarily geared toward guys that are naturally in their masculine, and women that are naturally in their feminine. It is for helping guys become who they are really meant to be. It's about becoming the man you really are inside.

I am talking about learning how to experience crazy, head over heels in love with the person you are with. When you have polarity, the guy is centered and in his masculinity, and the woman is in her femininity, they can't get enough of each other. That is the goal, to get people to that place, where they can have those kinds of relationships. It is not about just kind of hanging out and having a mediocre relationship.

There are couples out there where he is more of a feminine guy, and the woman is more of a masculine woman, and they have polarities that way. It tends to be rarer, and I would say that more than likely, those two people have a good understanding of relationships, where they own the essence of who they are. But the majority of people in society end up adopting a "mask", so to speak.

To give an example: Women, because they are in the workplace and career, have to take on this masculine mask so they can compete in the business world. Even as far as things have come – affirmative action and the whole nine yards, there is still a lack of equality in the marketplace. Many women, in order to adapt to that, take on a masculine mask. It also depends on how they were raised.

It is the same with guys. There are a lot of guys that are masculine at their core, but because of how they were raised and how they've associated different meanings to things, they take on a feminine mask, when they really are a masculine guy at heart.

So when you get these "masked" people that meet each other, well, it's like my friend I was telling you about. She is a very feminine woman, but she definitely wore a masculine mask, and that was how she was raised: *You have to grow up. You have to be successful. You have to have a career. You have to be driven.* She literally told me, *I was bred for success.*

When she was in her late 20s, she kept dating guys that were 10-15-20 years older than she is. All these guys wore a feminine mask, like her father had. She was never fulfilled, and never passionate, I mean *really* passionate about these guys, but that was part of the problem. Look what happened when she met a guy like me: I'm interested, she's beautiful, she's an amazing woman, but it was just too much work to be with her. She didn't know how to come out from behind the masculine mask.

Women find this, too. When they meet a guy that is a great guy, but he is too much into his feminine… well, nobody wants to have to fix the other person to make them into what they ideally want. There are people out there that try to fix people they get in relationships with and we all know that never works out.

It happens too often in society, so this book is about teaching guys to *own* the essence of who they are. That is the important thing. So if they are more of a feminine guy than they are a masculine guy, and they *own* that essence? They are going to go out and find a woman that is more in her masculine essence than she is in her feminine essence. And he's going to be really drawn to her, and they're going to have polarity, because he *owns* who he is, and because she owns who she is.

Become Comfortable Being Yourself

I am going to say this again, because it is such an important point to make: *When you* **own** *this material and you can live it, it* **becomes** *you.* You just own it. You just instinctively know, right away, where your lady's level of attraction is.

Even the guys that really understand women can't tell you specifically what you have to do. They just *own* their masculinity, they *own* their strength, and they *own* their core, their purpose and direction in life. They are naturally confident with women, because they grew up in a very loving household, or worked hard at discovering how to get to where they are at.

You become comfortable with being yourself. You make it part of who you are. Sooner or later you own it. And you **have** to own it, because if you can't maintain it later in the relationship, if you ever let it down, you will not be the person she thought you were in the first place. She will see weakness and test and pull away, causing you to start to pursue, which in turn drives her away even more.

One of the last things I want to mention here is about making lasting change. Why should a guy do these things? The simple answer is: *The definition of insanity is to continue doing the same things over and over again and expect to get different results.* You have to ask yourself: *Has what you have been doing in the dating world or your relationships in the past worked to the point where you have the type of relationship that you really know you deserve in your life?* Obviously if you are reading this book, then the answer is: *No.*

The Many Faces of Endings

Another thing that should be common sense is don't try to keep someone who doesn't want to keep you. In other words, don't pursue a woman who is not reciprocating a high level of attraction back at you. That is the cornerstone of all this information: *Always continue reading her level of attraction in you.*

Once a guy really understands women and is able to get into a relationship, they are going to realize, as I did, that every relationship is an opportunity for growth. Just because you absolutely adore and treasure the person you are with, doesn't mean you are going to spend the rest of your life with this person, or that you are going to marry her. You may start dating a woman and think for the first few months that this is your soulmate and you're going to spend the rest of your life together. In a true relationship, people either grow together, or they grow apart.

By understanding this information, you will at least be able to be in a relationship with someone you absolutely love, and treasure, and adore. They can help you become and understand the type of man you are totally capable of becoming. At the same time, you inspire and help her grow into everything she is capable of becoming as a woman.

That was what happened with my last girlfriend. She was from London, and to make a long story short, since this information was shared earlier in the book, it worked better for her to get her degree back in the U.K., than it did for her to get it here in the States.

It was basically why I told her I wanted to see other people. Since she is going to be going to school over there, I don't want to go from spending two to three months at a time with someone to seeing them for ten days every three months. It is not what I wanted.

When we ended our relationship, it was hard. It was hardest because we really, truly loved each other, but neither one of us was at the place where we were ready to get married. I made that mistake once when I was in my mid-20s. It's funny how life brings back around situations that are similar to those we experienced before. I would not want to make the same mistake with my ex-girlfriend from London. I love her, and I wouldn't change anything about her. She is a perfect woman.

One of the things I learned, because we talked a lot through this whole process of the break up, was how to end a relationship on a note of love. When a couple breaks up, often one person or both people walk away and hate each other, or are mean to each other. The great thing was that we loved each other so much, that we didn't want to lose what we had. The only thing we lost was the physical intimacy.

The Ten Disciplines of Love

A friend of mine went to a Tony Robbins event on relationships and shared some of her notes with me upon her return. The base information correlated so well with what I have been trying to share with you throughout this book, that I felt it made a wonderful summary of ways to deal with an on-going relationship. Below is a paraphrasing of those important concepts in the context of what I have already been teaching to you.

The ten disciplines of love are those things that you should focus on to keep the magic alive **after** she is in love with you. These are not things you do with somebody you just started dating. It is only after she has reached that magical 9-10 attraction level that you should start implementing these disciplines as a part of your relationship life. Her heart needs to be completely opened and engaged.

1. Discipline of Selflessness

- You go to a relationship to give
- Put your lover's needs first
- It is not about you
- It's about what you give not what you get
- When you are feeling pain you are focused on yourself.
- When you are feeling pain start focusing on the other person.

You are there to give to the other person in the relationship. It's not about you. You are just focused on giving, because that's who you are. You don't care about what comes in return. If you are feeling pain, thinking: *I'm doing this, I'm doing that for this person.* You are focused on what you're getting instead of what you are giving. You go to a relationship to give. You are not there to focus on what is coming in return.

If you are feeling pain in your relationship, it's a sign that you are not giving to your lover or your girlfriend, what you need to be giving. It means give her your presence. Make her laugh, show her a good time, take her out for fun, it means doing all the little things that make your partner happy.

2. Discipline of loving no matter what

- Withholding your gift is the only source of pain
- To withhold your gift is not to be who you really are
- With real love you will love through joy, pain, and fear because love penetrates everything.

When it talks about withholding your gift, if you have something to say and it's really bothering you, get it off your chest, but do it in a positive manner. If you have something you want to share, or tell your partner, just do it.

Guys who apply these concepts get to the point where they can just give of who they are and not worry about what is coming in return. When you want to share something and you hold it in, it becomes uncomfortable. You are afraid of giving or sharing, because you're afraid of how the other person is going to react. You need to just allow yourself to be who you are.

3. Discipline of being yourself

- Emanating and expressing your true essence and true core.
- Playing small never serves anybody.

You have to be the person you were meant to be. By holding things inside and sacrificing who you are to be someone you're not because you think that's what someone else wants of you, you will make neither person happy. The whole goal is to get to the place where you are comfortable being yourself, and you are indifferent and unaffected by all the tests your woman throws at you.

4. Discipline of presence and playfulness

- If you are a guy, be her mountain, nothing shakes you
- If you are a woman, be his joy, playfulness is the gift of life.

The man is a rock, the woman is his joy. Joy is the playfulness of love.

5. Discipline of positive intent

- Eliminate the threats and judgments and remember the power of language.
- Never make your partner wrong.
- Know their soul.
- People at their core are good. Evil is good gone wrong.
- You choose who you are at every moment.

Think about the words you are saying, and the effect it will have on your partner. Before you say anything, put yourself in your partner's shoes, and imagine how it would feel to have those things said to you. Don't argue with your girlfriend or your wife, because you are never going to win anyway.

6. Discipline of loving truth

- Vulnerability is power.
- Give the gift of heart-felt honesty and commit to expressing it openly in this moment.
- Don't let things build up.

To be a woman is to be feminine. It's being open and it's being receptive. That is very powerful. It is the true essence of who she is. For a guy being vulnerable is putting his self on the line, putting himself out there for potential rejection. You are expressing who you are inside, and while there is the potential for pain, there is also the potential for great pleasure in expressing who you are.

7. Discipline of freedom

- Power of forgiving, forgetting and flooding.
- Flooding yourself with positive emotions and feelings.
- Pain can only be found in yesterday's sorrows or tomorrow's concerns.
- Flood yourself now with the beauty and magic of your life

Flood yourself with positive emotions. Think about all of the good things in your life, past and present, and bring the feelings associated with these things into you. For all the wonderful things in your life, be grateful. For example: *Be grateful that you are reading this book and learning all of this wonderful information!*

8. Discipline of daily passion and intimacy

- Open your heart and hold nothing back
- Fear and hurt imprison the heart.
- Do the opposite of what they tell you and passion will grow. When she says "nothing's wrong" – dig deeper until you find out what that is.

What you fear, you attract. Fear is only an illusion.

9. Discipline of utilization

- Power of higher meaning spiritually and constant personal growth.
- There is a plan don't push against it but go with it.
- Find the good and beauty in everything and use it to expand your love.

Life is like floating down a stream. If you try to swim upstream, you are going against the current and will only wear yourself out. In other words, go with the flow!

10. Discipline of gratitude

- Appreciation is the power.
- Experience life's greatest blessings now.
- Be an appreciator of all good things you have in your life.

Conclusion

Once you master the understanding of women and feel your true center, it will spill over into other areas of your life. You will feel confident beyond anything you have ever felt before. You will feel more like a complete man and your inner strength that may have been somewhat dormant will come alive. This inner strength will cause you to strive to be more and to contribute more to yourself and others. You will have a feeling of peace and satisfaction because you now have a new understanding.

For me, it felt as though the chains on my heart were broken and I was able to become so much more of a man than I had ever dreamed of being. As you walk around and pay attention, you will start to notice how many people need this information. You may find yourself wanting to help those that want to be helped. Most importantly, living these principles of being a 3% man will unconsciously give permission to others to be like you.

People will start coming to you for advice because they will want to emulate your success with women. You become comfortable in your own skin and in being yourself. You will give your gifts to the world and your lady and will be indifferent to what comes in return. In other words, you are not attached to results and are not disappointed when a woman rejects you, has no interest in you, tests you, or when things do not work out the way you wanted them to.

You accept what has shown up in your life as the way it's supposed to be and simply make the choices that continue to move you in the direction of what you really want. When your lady tests you, you will see it coming and find it cute, because you know exactly how to pass her test with ease and have her come running back. Her tests are small and you pass them with ease. If you ever become complacent, you will recognize that her tests are becoming harder and instantly know what to do to turn it around.

You have become a 3% man.

If you know of anyone that you think may be interested in this book, or could benefit from what you have read here, please send them to my website, UnderstandingRelationships.com

If you have read this book and you really need some help integrating these concepts, or need some help to turn things around in your relationship fast, I also do one-on-one phone and Skype coaching on a first come first serve basis, as my schedule permits. You will find the information on phone and Skype coaching on my website at UnderstandingRelationships.com/products. I am happy to help you, and help any others to find the power in their lives that I have found in mine. I salute you for having the courage to take your power back, and become the person you were meant to be.

Made in the USA
Lexington, KY
23 March 2016